The Achievers

Great Women in the Biological Sciences

D1404948

Erica Stux

Avisson Press Inc.
Greensboro

First Edition
Printed in the USA
ISBN 1-888105-70-4

Library of Congress Cataloging-in-Publication Data

Stux, Erica.
   The Achievers : great women in the biological sciences / Erica
   Stux.— 1st ed.
      p. cm. — (Avisson young adult series)
   Includes bibliographical references and index.
   ISBN 1-888105-70-4 (tr. paper)
      1. Women life scientists—Biography—Juvenile literature.
      I. Title. II. Series.

QH305.5.S88 2005
570'.92'2—dc22
[B]
                                                    2004057087

Contents

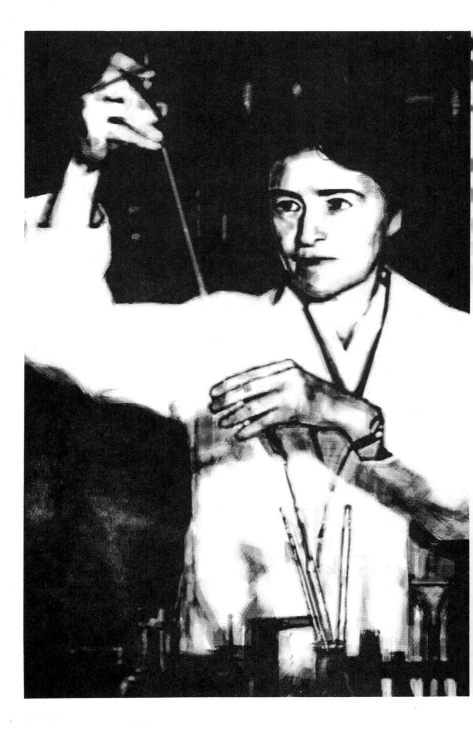

Gerty Cori

When Gerty Radnitz was born on August 15, 1896, nobody could have predicted that this girl from a wealthy Jewish family in central Europe would one day help unravel the puzzle of how the human body stores sugar and uses it for energy. Her work, in collaboration with her husband, would prove that understanding basic chemical processes that take place in living tissues is important to biology and medicine.

Gerty had a pleasant childhood in Prague, which was then part of the Austro-Hungarian Empire, but is now the capital of the Czech Republic. The oldest of three girls, she was tutored at home until she was ten. Her parents implanted in her, besides a love of learning, a love of outdoor activities. Her father Otto Radnitz was a chemist who managed several sugar-beet refineries. Like most fathers of his time, he sent his daughters to a finishing school, to prepare them to become charming wives and mothers. However, an uncle who was a pediatrician convinced Gerty she should go to medical school.

Getting into a medical school required a

knowledge of Latin, math, physics, and chemistry, none of which Gerty had studied. With remarkable determination, she set out to make up for her lack. During the summer of 1912, while the family was on vacation in the Austrian Alps, she met a teacher who agreed to tutor her in Latin. By the end of the summer, she had mastered the equivalent of three years of Latin. She enrolled in that teacher's school, and after a year she was ready to pass the medical school's entrance exam—"the hardest examination I was ever called upon to take."

In 1914, at eighteen, Gerty began her medical studies at the German branch of Carl Ferdinand University in Prague. She fell in love with the subject of biochemistry, an exciting new science that applied the principles of chemistry to problems of biology. She decided that she would devote herself to biochemical research.

In her anatomy class she met a tall blond young man named Carl Cori, and discovered that he enjoyed hiking, mountain climbing, and skiing just like she did. He also wanted to do research. Their personalities meshed well; he was shy, whereas she was vivacious and quick-witted. He thought Gerty was "a young woman who had charm, vitality, intelligence, a sense of humor, and love of the outdoors." They decided to marry, although Carl's family objected to Gerty's Jewish background; they felt it would hurt Carl's career. To resolve the problem, Gerty adopted Carl's Catholic religion. They were married in 1920, after Carl returned from serving in the Austrian army during World War I.

In post-war Europe, physicians were needed more than researchers. Gerty took a position at a hospital in Vienna, where she treated patients born with a thyroid deficiency. Her experiences with those patients resulted in the publication of several scientific papers. Carl meanwhile worked at the University of Graz, almost a hundred miles from Vienna. They spent weekends together, visiting Vienna's art museums or hiking through the countryside. Soon they arrived at a decision: they must leave Europe to find better research facilities.

An offer came from a cancer research center in Buffalo, New York, now called Roswell Park Memorial Institute, for Carl to join the staff. He sailed for America in 1922, leaving Gerty behind. Six months later he obtained for Gerty a position as assistant biochemist at the Institute. They would remain there for nine years.

Carl and Gerty were free to pursue their own interests, which were to gain an understanding of the complex processes that take place in the body.

They wanted to investigate how cancerous tumors use sugar for energy in order to grow. But first they had to understand how normal body tissues store and use sugar. Little was known at that time how the body can maintain a constant supply of energy. A French scientist had discovered that muscle and liver both contain a starch-like substance called glycogen, which breaks down into sugar. The hormone insulin had just been discovered in 1921 and was known to play a part in controlling the amount of sugar in the blood. But what was the relationship between glycogen and insulin?

For six years the Coris carried out experiments on laboratory rats. At one point the director of the Institute ordered Gerty to remain in her own lab and stop working with Carl. But they were determined to collaborate, so they ignored the order. They fed rats carefully measured amounts of sugar, and then examined what happened to the sugar when the rats were given insulin. Gerty developed the analytical methods that were needed.

The Coris discovered that after sugar enters the bloodstream, some of it is converted into energy, some is transformed into fat, and about half of it is converted into glycogen. Glycogen is stored in the liver and in muscles. When energy is needed, glycogen in the muscles is broken down into sugar.

The byproduct that is left after energy is extracted from the sugar is a simpler substance called lactic acid. This lactic acid is sent to the liver, where it is converted back into sugar. The bloodstream takes sugar back to the muscles, where it is stored in the form of glycogen. Thus there is a continuous recycling of the substances needed to provide energy. Insulin is needed to keep sugar in the blood within the proper range. This process became known as the Cori cycle.

During their years in Buffalo the Coris published fifty papers jointly. Gerty published eleven on her own, and Carl another thirty. Gerty was the lab genius, reading widely and getting ideas for new methods. Carl was more of a visionary; he took data and formed it into theories. Both were ambitious and highly motivated, and each trusted the other's work. Early in their careers, Carl realized that working with an independent woman like Gerty was "a delicate operation which requires much give and take on both sides and occasionally leads to friction, if both are equal partners and not willing to yield on a given point." This give-and-take, their mutual trust, and their deep affection made for a smooth-working team.

Even though they enjoyed their years in Buffalo, they decided they must leave their institute. They had made important discoveries and established scientific reputations, but they were not doing cancer research that the institute required. In order to continue their biochemical studies, they needed a more independent atmosphere.

Job offers came for Carl, but not for Gerty. He turned them down if the interviewers refused to hire Gerty as well. One interviewer told them it was downright un-American for a man to work with his wife. Many universities had a policy against hiring two in the same family. Gerty wanted not only a lab to work in with her husband, but also official recognition.

In 1931 Washington University in St. Louis, Missouri, offered positions to both Coris. Carl would head the department of pharmacology (the science of drugs), and Gerty would be a research assistant in the medical school. But first Carl was asked to give a lecture to the faculty. The lecture was well-received; only one faculty member opposed Carl's appointment. Carl paid a visit to this professor's anatomy lab, where bones were spread out everywhere. When Carl picked up a bone for a closer look, the professor asked if he could identify it. "It's the inner ear of a whale," Carl told him. The professor, suitably impressed, dropped his opposition.

Carl and Gerty found they had to make their own supply of biochemicals. Gerty controlled how they were made and stored, to insure their uniform quality. Her enthusiasm rubbed off on their student workers. She wanted every day to count, to bring them a little closer to a significant result. Anything less than perfection was not acceptable to Gerty. "Every experiment was a burning and exciting event," one graduate student recalled.

To understand biochemical processes, the Coris used minced frog muscle in their new experiments. They soaked the frog muscle in pure water and separated the cells, thus leaving water-soluble substances from muscle in the water. Analyzing this water, they discovered that glycogen breaks down into sugar in three steps. Gerty continued investigating these steps during her pregnancy. In 1936 she gave birth to their only child, Carl Thomas Cori. Three days later, she returned to the lab.

After full weekdays and a half-day of work on Saturday, the Coris relaxed at home. Sometimes they went swimming or skating, played tennis, or attended concerts. Frequently they entertained at home, mixing writers, artists, and business people with their scientific associates. Summer vacations were spent mountain climbing in Colorado or in Europe.

In their research, the Coris turned to a study of enzymes, which are substances that allow chemical reactions to take place without being changed themselves. Hormones act as enzymes by facilitating certain processes in living cells. Gerty in particular wanted to know what enzymes are involved in breaking down glycogen into sugar. She and Carl succeeded in isolating the enzyme that breaks the bonds holding hundreds of sugar molecules together in glycogen. At an international conference in 1939, Carl demonstrated that the enzyme could also tie the sugar molecules together to form glycogen. It was a dramatic moment when he passed around the test tube for everyone to see the starch-like material. This was the first time such a process had been carried out outside of a living cell.

Gerty and Carl's research led to the discovery of other enzymes. The conversion of glycogen to sugar and back turned out to be a multi-step process involving a number of enzymes. The direction of the reaction depends on the relative amounts of the components. A small amount of glycogen must be present in order for more of it to be formed. The level of glycogen never goes down to zero, due to the intervention of another enzyme that preserves the last traces of it.

The Coris explored how enzymes turn off or on any of the chemical steps they control. Their work began to explain the relationship between the structure of a substance and its function in the body. They showed that missing enzymes, or other mistakes in normal biochemistry, lead to a variety of diseases.

Gerty was the major contributor of seven of the ten papers the Coris published in 1938 and 1939. Although she attained a world reputation, Washington University still regarded her as a lowly research assistant. This changed during the years of World War II. Because of manpower shortages, women scientists were in demand. In 1944 Gerty was made an assistant professor, and in 1947, a full professor. Other universities tried to lure the Coris away, but when Washington University offered Carl the chairmanship of an enlarged biochemistry department, they decided to stay.

The Coris' lab became the worldwide center for the study of enzymes. Researchers came from all over to work for a year or two with them. By the early 1950s, Gerty was running the lab, while Carl kept busy writing and supervising other researchers. When not in the lab, Gerty read scientific journals. She convinced the university librarian to send new journals to her as soon as they arrived. She also read widely outside of science. A private library in St. Louis delivered half a dozen books to her office each week. By Friday she had finished them. All this reading gave her a broad knowledge of art, literature, sociology, and other subjects. Carl also had a wide range of knowledge. Lunch time at the lab was an education for the staff; talk ranged from recent scientific reports to the latest books the Coris had read.

Gerty was the lively, good-humored one of the couple. An exciting discovery sometimes made her jump and down. An interesting article might send her running down the hall to Carl's office to show him. But mistakes or lapses in others were not tolerated. When a researcher in Argentina discovered a new enzyme, she marched into the office of the associate working on a similar project, complaining "You missed it!" And when another associate ruined an experiment by forgetting to turn off a heater, she stormed "Haven't you any responsibility?" Her high standards and sharp tongue gave her a reputation as someone difficult to get along with. Yet she could be kind and caring. When one worker's babysitter quit, she sent her own housekeeper over to take charge. She helped visiting scientists find housing, and sometimes slipped money to young people in need.

Gerty was aware of discrimination against women scientists, and did her best to help young women in their careers. However, those who wore fashionable clothes she regarded with disapproval. She herself wore severe business suits to work. When writing a grant application to the Rockefeller Foundation, she made sure that she was included as an equal partner to Carl. Unfortunately, someone at the Rockefeller Foundation crossed out all references to "the Coris" and substituted "Dr. Cori" and "he". Gerty never knew about these changes; she would have been furious.

Washington University changed its rules of employment during the 1950s. Henceforth husbands and wives could both work at the university, but only if they were in different departments. But Gerty received a letter stating that she was exempt from the new rule. The university authorities had realized they could not separate the Coris.

In 1947 Gerty and Carl received both bad news and good news. While hiking in the Rocky Mountains that summer, Gerty fainted. They realized that the high altitude must have affected the oxygen-carrying ability of her blood. But her physician in St. Louis was unable to explain why that happened.

A few weeks later, the Coris were notified that they had won the Nobel Prize in Medicine and Physiology, sharing it with Bernardo A. Houssay of Argentina. Gerty would become the third woman scientist to win a Nobel. The next day reporters descended on their lab, but were astonished that both Coris went about their business as usual. Gerty, always a realist, felt that prestige is attached to the award rather than to the work that earned the award.

Before they left for Sweden for the Nobel ceremonies, they received the diagnosis of Gerty's condition. She had a rare form of anemia; her body was not producing red blood cells, and her bone marrow was being destroyed. Just when she was to gain worldwide recognition, she had to begin a struggle simply to survive.

The couple stuck to their plans as though nothing had happened. Their prize cited their discovery of the enzymes that convert glycogen to sugar and back again. "Your synthesis of glycogen in the test tube is beyond doubt one of the most brilliant achievements in modern biochemistry," the Nobel Committee stated. In their Nobel lecture, Carl delivered the first and third parts, and Gerty the second part. Carl's speech at the banquet thanked the committee for including his wife. That was "a source of deep satisfaction to me . . . Our efforts have been largely complementary, and one without the other would not have gone as far as in combination." He also expressed appreciation for the good fortune they found in the United States. "Our adopted country has treated us with the utmost generosity and has been of great importance for our scientific development and our outlook on life." Upon returning home, the Coris shared part of their prize money with several co-workers.

Gerty continued to work as before, in spite of her illness. She underwent periodic blood transfusions, often administered by Carl. She kept an army cot in her office, where she could rest whenever she felt the need. Although she never spoke of her illness, friends sensed the bitterness she kept bottled up.

After the Nobel Prize, other honors were heaped on Gerty. She was elected to the National Academy of Science, and appointed to the board of the newly-formed National Science Foundation. Other awards included the Sugar Research Prize, the Women's National Press Award, and several honorary degrees. She stated that the contributions she was able to make to science were due to "the benefits of two civilizations, a European education followed by the freedom and opportunities of this country."

Gerty's later projects involved sorting out a group of children's diseases called glycogen storage disorders. She thought that one particular enzyme was missing in those children. A co-worker thought it was another enzyme that was missing. It turned out both were right. Each missing enzyme causes a different form of the disease. Gerty eventually showed that four related diseases are caused by the absence of particular enzymes. Since her work, other glycogen storage diseases have been described. But Gerty Cori opened up the entire field of genetic diseases. A co-worker wrote "It is hard to imagine how revolutionary her accomplishment was—that someone could take a piece of liver . . . from a patient and determine what was wrong with them and why they had particular symptoms. It was a major finding, really a milestone in biochemistry and our understanding of a whole category of diseases."

In the fall of 1957, Gerty became bedridden. No more an avid reader, her reading was now limited to mysteries. On October 26 she died, at the age of sixty-one. Carl lived another twenty-seven years, and eventually married again.

Late in her life, Gerty expressed her philosophy: "I believe that the wonder of the human spirit is expressed in art and science. I see no conflict between the two. Honesty, intellectual integrity, courage, and kindness are the virtues that I admire. Love of my work and devotion to it are for me the basis of happiness." She remained true to this philosophy to the end.

Josephine Baker

Sara Josephine Baker was as proud of her new outfit as any six-year-old could be. She loved the white lace dress with a blue sash, the light blue silk stockings, and the matching shoes. While she waited for her mother to come downstairs, she wandered out to the sidewalk, wondering if anyone would come by and admire her clothes.

Someone did come by—a little black girl in a ragged dress. The two eyed each other. Suddenly conscious of the disparity between them, Sara Josephine took off her dress, her shoes, and even her underwear. She handed them to the other girl, who scampered off in delight. Then she went inside to tell her mother what she had done. She was thankful that her mother was not angry.

This urge to set things right in situations that seemed to require action stayed with Josephine all her life. Because of her accomplishments, cities became much healthier places to live.

Josephine was born on November 15, 1873, in Poughkeepsie, New York. Called Jo by her family, she was the third of four children of a well-to-do lawyer. During her childhood, she enjoyed family picnics, fishing trips, boat trips, baseball games, and frequent parties. In fall and winter, hayrides and ice skating offered recreation. Among the children there was no need for chores because servants took care of all household jobs.

Jo attended the Misses Thomas' School for Young Ladies, an experimental school with informal classes, where she learned to set her own goals. The education she received there was meant to prepare her for college studies at Vassar, the women's college located in Poughkeepsie.

In the spring of 1890, when Jo was sixteen, her idyllic life came to an end. Her beloved brother died of typhoid fever at the age of thirteen. Shortly thereafter, her father also died of typhoid. This prompted Josephine to decide to study medicine. A medical career, besides helping sick people, would also help Josephine support her mother and her one living sister.

Typhoid fever was a major health problem in the late 1800s and early 1900s. It resulted in high fever, intense headaches, delirium, and often death. Other widespread serious diseases were tuberculosis, smallpox, and dysentery. These were especially common in young children. Doctors did not know how to cure those diseases, or what caused them. Antibiotics were still unknown.

Poor hygiene and poor sanitation in the cities contributed to the spread of disease. Unpasteurized milk was sold from dirty open cans. Dead horses or dogs were left lying in the streets to rot. Sewage often flowed through open gutters. Many babies did not live past their first birthday. In the slum areas of New York City, 1500 babies died every week in the summer of 1902, mostly from dysentery.

Around the turn of the century, there were very few women doctors, but Josephine was determined to join their ranks. She persuaded her mother to pay the $5000 cost of medical school. But first she had to study a number of courses, especially science, in order to pass the entrance exam. After a year of independent study, she was ready for medical school.

At twenty she enrolled at the Women's Medical College of the New York Infirmary for Women and Children—the only school she knew of that would accept women. At first the work was very difficult for her, but she studied hard, and in the end ranked second in her graduating class. One course on "The Normal Child", which she had to repeat, became the basis of her future work.

After earning her medical degree, Josephine

interned at the New England Hospital for Women and Children in Boston. She also worked at a clinic in a slum area of Boston. She was appalled at the misery she saw there, due to overcrowding and lack of sanitation. It was little wonder that diseases spread rapidly among the slum residents.

In 1900 Josephine and a medical school classmate opened their medical office in New York City. But few patients came. To make extra money, the two took jobs as medical examiners for two life insurance companies. But first they had to persuade the company officials of the advantage of having women medical examiners. Now the two doctors at least had a steady income.

The following year, Josephine took a job with the city's Health Department as a medical inspector. Her work at first involved visiting public schools to examine children. Any child that was sick, had an eye infection or head lice, was sent home. But truant officers often sent the sick child back to school. Josephine was allowed one hour at each of three or four schools per day.

Josephine had the Department of Health establish a city-wide school nurse program. It was so successful that head lice and eye infections, once prevalent in the schools, were almost totally eradicated.

Next, the Department of Health sent Josephine into the slums to find sick babies. All day long, she climbed stairs in countless crowded buildings. The rooms were hot and smelled of sour milk. Flies buzzed at the windows. Everywhere she faced hostile men and tired-looking women who seemed to accept the fact that some of their babies would die. On a typical day, she entered an apartment after climbing to the fourth or fifth floor. In the dim light, she saw a thin woman lying on a mattress in a corner. Beside the woman, hidden in the folds of a blanket, was the small form of a baby.

She set down her doctor's bag and uncovered the baby. "It's too late," the young mother said wearily. "He's gone, isn't he?" Josephine nodded. Sadly she picked up her bag and left. One more dead baby to add to the statistics. But why did they have to die?

Josephine realized that many of these deaths could be prevented. "By the time I see the babies, or by the time the mother calls for a doctor, it's too late," she told her boss Dr. Bensel. "We must teach the mothers how to keep their babies well. After school is out for the summer, I'd like to use the school nurses. A nurse can visit every family that has a new baby, and tell the mother what she must do."

The Department of Health agreed to the plan.

Thirty school nurses began visiting families in one small area of New York City. New mothers were told that babies need fresh air, daily bathing, thin clothing in the summer, and proper feeding. At the end of that summer of 1908, deaths among babies had been cut by 1200 over the number of the previous summer. Josephine Baker's plan was a success! City leaders were so pleased that they gave her a budget to use on a disease prevention program.

Josephine was then made supervisor of a new city Department of Child Hygiene—the first woman in the United States to hold such an important post. But six male medical inspectors assigned to her department promptly resigned. They considered it a disgrace to have a woman as their boss. She persuaded them to stay for at least a month. At the end of the month, all six had changed their minds, and stayed on permanently.

Josephine's next project was to set up "milk stations", where nurses sold low-price baby formula, advised new mothers, and gave babies medical check-ups. At first, city leaders were not willing to fund this project. Josephine then approached a wealthy woman, Mrs. J. Borden Harriman, who was known to be interested in children's health. Mrs. Harriman and her friends raised enough money to pay for thirty milk stations. At first mothers were slow to bring their babies, but as confidence spread, women became more willing to come. The thirty stations helped more than 60,000 babies stay healthy.

Many babies at that time were delivered by women called midwives instead of doctors. Josephine carried on a long battle to have midwives licensed by the city. She organized a training program for them; those that completed the course were granted a license. This project also led to fewer deaths among newborn babies.

One of the things a midwife had to know was the proper use of eyedrops. Sometimes a baby is born with an eye infection that could lead to blindness. Drops of a silver nitrate solution are administered to a newborn's eyes to prevent this. But the solution a midwife used may have been contaminated, or have evaporated to a dangerous concentration. Josephine developed a foolproof dispenser for the solution: enough for each eye was sealed into a beeswax capsule. Cases of baby blindness decreased dramatically.

Josephine also turned her attention to the design of sensible clothing for babies. Her recommendations resulted in new clothing patterns offered by the McCall's Pattern Company.

Babies were often left in the care of an older sister, too young and inexperienced for the job. Josephine decided that girls needed to be taught how to be good babysitters. She organized a "Little Mother's League", a club to teach girls basic baby care. Girls in the elementary schools took to learning these lessons quickly and eagerly. They were proud to wear a badge that showed they had learned how to be a babysitter. They passed their knowledge on to their mothers, and reminded the mothers to go to their neighborhood milk station.

As a result of the publicity on the Little Mother's League, letters arrived from many foreign countries. People there wanted to know how to set up their own programs. Of course, Josephine was happy to give advice.

All these innovations reduced the death rate among babies, but Josephine Baker was still not satisfied. She wondered why so many died in orphanages. She decided what was missing in those babies' lives was good old-fashioned mothering. She took babies out of orphanages and placed them with families that would give them plenty of love. The results were amazing! That group of babies did much better than those left in orphanages or hospitals. As a result of this experiment, it became widespread practice to hold and rock babies that have to be confined to a hospital, either by nurses or by family members.

Dr. Baker was the first to recognize that babies need to be held and talked to.

One of Josephine Baker's triumphs was finding and apprehending the woman known as Typhoid Mary. From 1900 to 1907, seven New York families had suffered from multiple cases of typhoid fever. An investigation by the Department of Health found that all seven families had employed a cook named Mary Mallon. Dr. Baker went to find Mary and take specimens of her body fluids. But when she arrived at the house, the door was slammed in her face. She returned with several policemen. Mary again tried to slam the door, but a policeman's foot was planted in the doorway. Mary ran into the house, but could not be found by the policemen. Then Dr. Baker noticed a chair by a backyard fence, and footprints in the snow. The policemen found Mary next door, cowering in a closet. She fought off all attempts to have a blood sample taken, so she was transported to a nearby hospital. Samples taken there were found to contain huge numbers of typhoid germs. She was kept at the hospital for almost three years, but all efforts to rid her body of the germs failed. She was finally released, on the condition that she return every three months for testing, and never take up cooking for others again. She disappeared into the slums of New York, and the Health Department lost track of her. Five years later, when new cases of typhoid arose, Mary was found again. She was taken into custody without a struggle, and quarantined on a small island. There she remained as a guest of New York City, until her death twenty-three years later.

In spite of all the good Dr. Baker was doing, she made enemies. Some doctors actually protested that her innovations were bad for the medical field. Thirty doctors signed a petition sent to the mayor of New York, asking that the Bureau of Child Hygiene be abolished. "It was ruining medical practice by its results of keeping babies well", the petition stated. Dr. Baker responded in a letter to the mayor, "This is the first compliment I've received since the Bureau of Child Hygiene was established." The petition was quickly forgotten. Another doctor complained that "if we're going to save the lives of all the women and children at public expense, what incentive will there be for a young man to go into medicine?" In view of the sophisticated diagnostic tools and other medical advances that have been made, this seems like a laughable attitude today.

Discrimination was also rampant at New York University, where Dr. Baker gave a lecture on child hygiene each year, from 1915 to 1930. Men students did not like being taught by a woman, and did their best to disrupt her lectures. She ignored them as much as she could. As a result of having Dr. Baker lecture its students, the university was forced to admit women into its degree program.

In 1914 an invitation came to "Dr. S. J. Baker" to speak to the Philadelphia College of Physicians. Some of the physicians were surprised to discover that Dr. S. J. Baker was a woman. The college president, in introducing her before her speech, noted that no woman had been allowed in the building since the college was founded in 1787.

In 1919 there was again a movement to remove Dr. Baker from her post, by those who resented having a woman in charge of a city bureau. But the public rallied around her in support. Mothers whose babies probably owed their lives to Dr. Baker marched to the mayor's office in protest. The local press also published editorials declaring that should she should not be dismissed.

During the flu epidemic of 1918, when other cities were closing their schools, Dr. Baker convinced city officials that New York schools should stay open. School would be the safest place for children, she argued. At the end of the epidemic, it was found that school-age children in New York had suffered the least, compared to other groups. Dr. Baker had been right again.

Josephine had been carrying on a private practice in addition to her work for the city. When an election changed the city's leadership, city employees were ordered to give up their outside work, or else quit their job. Josephine chose to remain with the city Health Department. But, like other city employees, she had to take a civil service exam to prove her fitness for her position. The exam proved to be quite difficult, but she passed it with flying colors.

Public health and medicine were not Josephine's only interests. She was an active suffragette, working to give women the right to vote. Often she stopped at a street corner to talk to passersby about the importance of letting women have a say in elections. A male audience always included hecklers, but she learned to talk back to them. When a women's suffrage parade was organized, Josephine was among the 500 women marchers. Each year the parade grew larger; hundreds of men also joined the women. Josephine was then invited to be part of a delegation that was to meet with President Woodrow Wilson at the White House. The women were pleased that President Wilson pledged his support in granting women the right to vote. "As we went back to New York, we all felt that our fight had finally been won there in the White House reception room", Josephine recalled later. Women's right to vote was achieved in 1920, when Congress passed the 19th amendment to the Constitution.

Dr. Baker was recognized as the world's leading expert on children's health. She traveled all over the country, as well as overseas, giving talks on that subject. Health officials came from all over the world to consult her. She wanted every state of the United States to set up a children's health agency, and by 1923 they all did. Other cities tried to hire her away, but she was devoted to New York. "To consider leaving it was like considering an operation that would completely change my personality" she wrote.

As a determined crusader, Josephine Baker developed her own standards of preventive medicine, and saw them widely adopted. She served as president of the American Child Hygiene Association, and after her retirement, of the American Medical Women's Association. During her later years she published five books, and almost two hundred articles, most of them in popular periodicals. She also served on the Health Committee of the League of Nations—the forerunner of the United Nations. Lecturing and consulting kept her busy after her official retirement. The lectures often touched on women's rights as well as children's. Her final years were spent on a farm in New Jersey that was home to retired professional women. There she wrote her autobiography, titled *Fighting For Life*, which was published in 1939. She died of cancer in 1945, at the age of seventy-one.

When Josephine Baker began her work in New York, one out of every six babies died before its first birthday. After twenty-one years in the city health department, the rate was about one in eighteen. If she were alive today, Dr. Baker would be pleased to know that now only about one baby out of a hundred does not live till its first birthday.

Rita Levi-Montalcini

Rita Levi-Montalcini's parents were under the influence of the Victorian era of the 19th century. That meant that the father made all decisions and controlled all aspects of family life. Girls were expected to become wives and mothers, and held an inferior place in society.

Rita was a shy, timid child, afraid of adults, especially her father. She always felt much closer to her mother. Yet it was her father who influenced the course her life was to take. From him she inherited seriousness and dedication to work. These characteristics, along with persistence and the joy of making discoveries, led her to make important contributions to the understanding of the processes in living beings.

Rita and her twin sister Paola were born on April 22, 1909, in Turin, Italy, the youngest of four children. Their father Adamo Levi was an electrical engineer; their mother Adele Montalcini was a talented painter. As young children, Rita and Paola were taken by their nanny on afternoon walks to a park. Local children met playmates there, while their nannies watched them play. Children were instructed to ask those they did not yet know their name, their father's profession, and their religion. Rita had no trouble answering the first two questions, but the third left her stumped. She asked her father. "You children are freethinkers," he instructed her. "If anyone asks, that is what you should say." Although not practicing any religion, the Levi family was Jewish. The question of religion was for a long time a source of discomfort and indecision to Rita.

The Levi children attended a public school because their parents wanted them exposed to children of all social classes. There Rita was instilled with patriotism, especially love for the Italian king and queen. After four years of elementary school came middle school. Mr. Levi decreed that his daughters would attend a girls' middle school and high school; these did not prepare anyone for university studies. To support his decision, he pointed to his two sisters, who had earned advanced degrees, but then had trouble reconciling their education with the duties of a wife and mother.

Paola and their older sister Nina accepted their father's decision. Their interests lay in the arts. Paola eventually became a painter, and Nina a writer. Rita, on the other hand, felt empty and isolated after finishing high school. She rejected the subordinate role expected of females of that time, and her natural shyness prevented her from reaching out to others. Reading books by the Bronte sisters and by Selma Lagerlof partially filled the emptiness in her life.

It was when the children's beloved nanny Giovanna was diagnosed with stomach cancer that Rita decided to study medicine. Her father's response to her hesitant announcement was "If this is really what you want, I won't stand in your way, even if I'm very doubtful about your choice."

Rita enlisted her cousin Eugenia to join her in preparation for university studies. Two teachers were hired to tutor them, one in Latin and Greek, the other in math. After eight months they felt ready to take the university entrance exam. Both girls passed with flying colors.

They enrolled in the Turin School of Medicine in the fall of 1930. They were among only seven young women in the first and second year classes. Rita passed her first year exams with honors. In her second year, she was among those chosen to be interns in the School of Anatomy. As interns, they were to prepare microscope slides of certain animal tissues, and count the cells in clusters of nerve cells from mice. The latter task seemed both tedious and useless to Rita and the others. A subsequent project was more to her liking: the study of nerve cells grown in a test tube—that is, outside a living body. Rita became enthusiastic about research of this sort. She learned a technique of staining nerve cells to bring out details—a technique that was to be useful to her in future research. Also, she and her professor, an eminent scientist named Giuseppe Levi, grew in admiration and affection, which lasted until his death.

As a university student, Rita was serious-minded, and not apt to make friends with fellow students, although a few tried to overcome the barrier she erected around herself. One male classmate initiated a relationship which blossomed into love on his part. Rita, though fond of him, felt their temperaments and interests were too different to consider marriage. Three years after their graduation, she was saddened to learn that he had died of tuberculosis.

The Italian government in the 1930s was headed by the dictator Benito Mussolini. Since seizing the reins of government in 1922, Mussolini had slowly consolidated his power by kidnapping and murdering his opponents. Mussolini's form of government, called fascism, proceeded to erode the personal freedom of its citizens. Opposition parties were disbanded, and the press was allowed to print only items supporting the fascist government. The Jewish population of Italy was hit especially hard by government decrees. They were dismissed from all public and academic positions, and deprived of their citizenship. In this respect, Italy followed the lead of its ally Germany. That country, under the dictator Adolf Hitler, passed increasingly repressive laws of persecution against Jews, culminating in the notorious death camps, where millions died.

Rita and her family read reports and propaganda pieces in the newspapers with disbelief and alarm. For the first time in her life, she felt proud of being Jewish; she became conscious of a bond with individuals vilified in the Italian press, and with Jewish victims of earlier massacres in eastern Europe.

In the fall of 1938, Rita was employed as assistant in Turin's Clinic for Nervous and Mental Diseases. She conducted research in neurology, specifically the activity of nerve centers in chick embryos. This presumably could shed light on the workings of the human nervous system. The result of her study was presented to an Italian journal, which rejected it because publication of articles by Jewish scientists was no longer allowed.. However, it was later published by a Swiss journal.

Among Rita's coworkers, there was no hint of hostility towards her. Yet an air of suspicion colored all professional relationships, for one never knew who might be an informer, ready to denounce someone to the authorities for something he or she had said.

In March 1939, Rita accepted an invitation to join a neurological institute in Brussels, Belgium. An added attraction in Brussels was the presence of her sister Nina, Nina's husband, and their three children. On weekends Rita traveled to Liege, a Belgian city near the German border, where her former professor Giuseppe Levi was then working, after being dismissed from the university.

In September of that year, everyone was horrified to learn of Germany's invasion of Poland, which marked the beginning of World War II. Foreseeing a German invasion of Belgium, Rita, along with Nina and her family, returned to Italy.

Since Rita could no longer attend any university institutes, a friend from medical school suggested in the fall of 1940 that she set up a small laboratory in her home, to continue her interrupted research. Rita embraced the idea eagerly. Chick embryos could be readily obtained. Her mother and siblings agreed to her setting up a lab in her bedroom. She began acquiring equipment she would need.

Her brother Gino built a glass heat-regulated box with two round opening for her arms. In this box she could operate on the embryos under a microscope. She transformed ordinary sewing needles into fine scalpels by grinding the points. Her first experiments in the spring of 1941 turned out well. By cutting off limbs not yet provided with nerves, she studied how this affected the development of cells in the spinal cord, and in nerve centers, during the very early stages of the embryo.

A scientific paper she read on a train trip during the summer of 1940 determined the course of her research. The author of this paper, Viktor Hamburger, had proposed the presence of a substance that makes cells in an embryo differentiate into motor neurons and sensory neurons. (Sensory neurons are nerve cells that send messages to the brain; motor neurons are nerve cells that send messages from the brain to specific muscles.) Rita decided to repeat Hamburger's work and perhaps extend it.

Giuseppe Levi returned to Turin from Liege, which was now controlled by the Germans. Rita asked him to join her in her research, which he did.

Thus, while the German army advanced in Russia and the Allied armies advanced in North Africa and the Italian island of Sicily, Rita and her former professor, in the refuge of her bedroom, examined three-day-old chick embryos whose budding limbs had been surgically removed.

How they could concentrate on this work while all around them death and destruction was being spread on land and from the air was remarkable. Rita later wrote that being fully aware of the war news would be too depressing. One's reaction must be to ignore the reality of the situation.

Life in Turin soon became too dangerous because of bombing raids. Whenever the siren announced the approach of bombers, Rita gathered up her precious microscope and slides of stained embryo tissues, and rushed down into the basement until the siren sounded the "all clear" signal.

In the fall of 1942, the family decided to move out of town to a small house an hour's drive away. In a corner of the living/dining room, Rita set up her small laboratory. She bicycled from farm to farm, asking for eggs for her experiments. After extracting embryos, she took the eggs into the kitchen for the family's future meals.

In spite of intermittent power failures, Rita completed several projects. Outdoors, she enjoyed watching nature unfold in the spring of 1943, something she was usually unaware of in the city. Her observations of birds and insects stimulated her interest in the nervous system, and shaped her thinking about how cells adapt to various functions in living beings.

That summer, on July 25, Mussolini resigned as head of the government. People rejoiced and hugged one another as the news spread. Only the Jewish population was apprehensive, for German troops were poised on the border, ready to take over Italy, just as they had other European countries.

When German tanks appeared in Turin, Rita and her family knew they had to flee. But where should they go? The border with Switzerland was already patrolled by German guards. They decided to go south, perhaps as far as the southern coast, where Allied troops had already gained a foothold on Italian soil. However, they got off the train in Florence, where Paola had a friend. The friend's mother agreed to rent them rooms, provided they were not Jewish. They assured her they were Catholic, as shown on their false identity cards. Later they found out that the woman realized from the beginning their true identity, but decided to go along with their deception.

Not being able to work, Rita, with Paola's help,

turned to making false identity cards for others. These were necessary for some individuals in order to obtain food rations.

In August 1944, war came to the streets of Florence. Snipers fired from rooftops at people below. From her window, Rita watched people fleeing from the German army. Soon, however, the German army was driven out by the Allied army that had slowly fought its way northward.

Rita presented herself to the Allies' health services and was assigned to an old military barracks that now served as a collection center for refugees pouring in from the surrounding countryside. She was to check each person's health and see them settled into a partitioned-off place in the barracks. The widespread malnutrition, especially among babies already close to death, saddened her. Overcrowding among the refugees then brought on an epidemic of typhoid fever, caused by drinking polluted water.

Rita felt powerless in treating the typhoid patients. She found she could not remain emotionally detached while facing so much misery. This led to her later decision not to be a practicing physician, but a researcher.

The end of the war saw Rita returning to Turin, where she resumed her previous position as assistant to Professor Levi. In July 1946 a letter from Viktor Hamburger arrived, asking Rita to come to Washington University in St. Louis, Missouri, where Hamburger was chairman of the zoology department. Together they could continue their investigation of the effect of tissues on the development of nerve fibers.

In September 1946 Rita sailed from the port of Genoa to New York. A luxurious train then took her to St. Louis — so different from the cattle cars she had traveled in during the war. The single semester she had planned to stay in St. Louis was to stretch out to thirty years.

A former student of Hamburger's named Elmer Bueker published a paper about his experiments, which also dealt with the characteristics of growing nerve cells. He had grafted a mouse tumor onto the body of a chick embryo. Tumors were known to grow rapidly, and the chick embryos at that stage did not reject them as foreign tissue. Bueker found that nerve fibers grew into the tumor; evidently the tumor provided a favorable environment for further growth of the nerves.

Rita, excited about these results, set to work to repeat Bueker's experiment. She found that the tumors became penetrated from all sides by nerve fibers, like dark rivers flowing between land masses. Immediately she had the feeling that something important was going on in those tissues. In tumors transplanted into three-day-old embryos, they were invaded within days after transplant by a thick network of nerve fibers. Other organs of the chick embryo were also rapidly invaded by nerve cells. The same thing happened even when there was no direct contact between the two types of tissues. This seemed to indicate that the tumors had released a substance that accelerated the growth of nerve fibers to an abnormal extent. The substance became known as nerve growth factor, or NGF.

Rita presented her results in a talk at the New York Academy of Sciences. Then she turned to a new technique—tissue culture—that is, growing tissues in lab dishes—to learn more about the strange substance in tumors that attracted nerve fibers. This technique would allow her to complete experiments in hours rather than weeks.

Rita's friend Hertha Meyer, a former co-worker of Professor Levi, was working in Rio de Janeiro, Brazil, and had set up a culture unit at her laboratory. Rita wrote to her to ask whether she might come to Rio and work there for several months. Permission was given, a grant was obtained to cover her travel expenses, and so in September 1952, Rita boarded a plane to Brazil. In her coat pocket was a box containing two live mice with the type of tumors she needed.

In her experiments in Rio, Rita found that normal mouse tissue had the same effect as tumors. So what was so special about the tumors? The "mouse effect" was not explained till many years later.

Her last month in Rio was spent in exploring the city and its surroundings. She was impressed by the mingling of various races, so different from the recent racist ideologies of Europe and even the separatism in the American South. After quick sightseeing trips to Peru and Ecuador, Rita returned to St. Louis in January 1953.

Hamburger had offered a young biochemist named Stanley Cohen a position on their research team. For the next several years, Rita and Stan would get together several times a day to discuss their work. It was a collaboration made in heaven. Stan knew biochemistry, Rita knew the nervous system. "You and I are good," Stan told her, "But together we are wonderful!" The years with Stanley Rita considered the most intense and productive of her life.

To provide Stan with enough of the strange growth-promoting substance, Rita had to extract it from dozens of tumors. Stanley then discovered that the salivary glands of mice contained more

NGF than the tumors. Besides that, an extract from salivary glands was found to contain a general growth factor, capable of acting on a large variety of cells. This substance became known as epidermal growth factor, or EGF.

Because of budget cutbacks, Stanley Cohen had to leave his position after six-and-a-half years of collaboration with Rita. After a sorrowful parting, the thought of continuing her work alone filled Rita with anxiety.

Since 1958 she had been a full professor at Washington University. For a long time, she had thought of establishing a research unit in Italy. The university agreed to her leaving for three months every year. In Rome, she was given three large rooms in the Institute of Health, fully equipped with all the instruments she would need.

Soon she was dividing her time equally between the laboratories on two continents. In both, the focus of research was the structure and range of action of the nerve growth factor. In moving from one place to the other, Rita had to adjust from the breezy cordiality among the St. Louis staff to the formality that governed relations between Italian professors and their students and technicians. But she always felt free to speak her mind, even if it meant calling another person stupid. Her months in

Italy allowed her to spend time with her mother before Mrs. Levi's death in 1963.

The National Research Council of Italy, which provided funding for Rita's Center of Neurobiology, expanded it in 1969 into a Laboratory of Cell Biology, of which Rita became the director. However, in the late 1970s the Research Council's interest in neurobiology waned. Italian researchers did not have the team spirit of Americans, and were free to pursue other paths of research rather than those assigned to them. Not being under pressure to publish, like American scientists, the Italians often took on risky projects which would, more often than not, lead nowhere.

Rita retired as director in 1979, but continued to work as a guest researcher. Other laboratories took up the study of NGF, using better equipment. One of the results was the identification of the gene that directs the production of NGF in mice and in humans. In ensuing years, other chemical messengers were discovered. It became possible to produce NGF in great quantities, to be used to treat dysfunctions of nerve circuits in human patients. EGF can also be used in clinical medicine—for example, to promote the healing of burns.

In 1986, Rita Levi-Montalcini and Stanley Cohen were awarded the Nobel Prize in Medicine and

Physiology in recognition of their discovery of NGF and EGF. She already had several other awards. Three years later she died in Rome.

In her autobiography, Rita wrote "In scientific work, neither the degree of one's intelligence nor the ability to carry out one's tasks with thoroughness and precision are factors essential to personal success and fulfillment. More important for the attaining of both ends are total dedication and a tendency to underestimate difficulties, which cause one to tackle problems that other, more critical and acute persons instead opt to avoid." It was this dedication and courage to take on difficult problems that led Rita Levi-Montalcini to her success as a researcher, and eventually to the Nobel Prize.

Rosalyn Yalow

Young Rosalyn Sussman climbed out of the window of her grandmother's apartment, onto the flat roof just outside. This was a place where she could read undisturbed. Reading was her favorite activity; it was a way to gain new knowledge. In this she was encouraged by her parents, who had never gone past elementary school themselves. They valued education, and expected Rosalyn and her older brother Alexander to do well at school.

Rosalyn's love of learning and her aptitude for mathematics steered her eventually to the study of physics. Her application of physics to medicine led to a remarkable discovery, which would have a far-reaching effect on the practice of medicine.

Rosalyn was born on July 19, 1921, in New York City. Her father Simon Sussman was also born there, and her mother Clara came to America from Germany at age four. The family owned a small paper and twine business. Rosalyn could read even before starting kindergarten. Her brother took her to the neighborhood public library every week, so that each would have new books to read.

From an early age, Rosalyn was a determined child, who always knew what she wanted, and insisted on having her own way. When money got tight in 1929, she helped her mother, who took in sewing from a neckwear company; as her mother sewed, Rosalyn turned the collars for her. It was a way of working towards a goal—a habit that Rosalyn learned to follow single-mindedly.

At school, Rosalyn loved her math classes. Already looking towards her future, at eleven, she announced to a twenty-four-year-old cousin, "When I'm your age, I'll have a doctor's degree already." At Walton High School, a teacher got her excited about chemistry. She knew she wanted to be a scientist, but which branch of science should she concentrate on? Years later, Rosalyn stated, "I went into science because I loved it, and I wasn't very good at anything else." But in addition to having a career, she always knew she would marry and have children. In the 1930s, it was quite unusual for a woman to do both.

After graduating from Walton at fifteen, Rosalyn enrolled at New York's Hunter College, an all-women's college with no tuition. There she took her first physics course, and promptly fell in love with the subject. She was further influenced by reading a biography of Marie Curie, the

Polish/French scientist who had won two Nobel Prizes, one in physics and one in chemistry. When the physicist Enrico Fermi arrived at Hunter to deliver a series of lectures, that clinched Rosalyn's decision to become a physicist.

The 1930s was an exciting time for physics. Radioactivity had been discovered—that is, the ability of certain chemical elements to give off energy spontaneously. Scientists were closing in on the internal structure of atoms—the basic building blocks of all substances. Fermi had been successful in inducing radioactivity artificially.

Although Rosalyn's family, being more practical, thought she should become a school teacher, Rosalyn persisted in her desire. Hunter College established a new physics degree program just for her. But in applying to graduate schools to continue her education, Rosalyn encountered double discrimination: she was a woman, and she was Jewish. In those days, most schools had quotas for Jewish students. However, one of her professors obtained a position for her as a secretary at Columbia University. This was to be a back-door entry into the graduate school, for employees were allowed to take courses at the university. There was only one hitch: she had to learn shorthand first.

Dutifully, she took a class in shorthand during her

senior year, and started the secretarial job after her graduation in January 1941. As it turned out, she did not stay there long. Less than two months later an offer arrived from the University of Illinois, one of the graduate schools to which she had applied. She could become a teaching assistant, starting the following September, teaching an undergraduate course while taking graduate courses.

She arrived at the University of Illinois and found herself the only woman among four hundred faculty members in the College of Engineering.. She was told she was the first woman in the department since 1917. Many young men were being drafted into military service, even though the United States had not yet entered World War II. Their departure opened up opportunities for women.

Rosalyn soon realized she not academically prepared for the graduate courses in physics. She had to take two undergraduate courses, which carried no credit, as well as three graduate courses. In addition, she taught a freshman course in physics. Since she had never taught before, she sat in on another instructor's classes, to observe how one goes about teaching. In December of that year, when the U.S. entered the war, many faculty members in the Engineering Department left to do scientific work for the government. This gave the remaining faculty a greater teaching load.

Rosalyn worked very hard, partly to show that a woman could do as well as any man. She received an A in all her courses, except for an A- in a lab course. That A- caused the department chairman to remark that it proved women were not cut out to do lab work. Besides good grades, Rosalyn acquired a boyfriend. Aaron Yalow was also a graduate student in physics, and the son of a rabbi. The two were married in 1943.

In January 1945 Rosalyn received her doctor's degree in nuclear physics. She returned to New York to take a position as assistant engineer at Federal Telecommunications Laboratory. Aaron remained in Illinois to finish work on his degree. He joined her in September of that year, and they set up housekeeping, first in an apartment in Manhattan, then a small house in the Bronx.

Aaron understood that Rosalyn would never let anything stand in the way of her career. He was a scientist too, but never in competition with his wife. He felt secure enough that he did not mind if Rosalyn were to surpass him professionally. Aaron's religion, rather than science, was the center of his life. Their marriage was based on an unspoken agreement: she would honor his religious requirements, and he would make no demands that interfered with her work. He became her greatest admirer.

When her research group left New York, Rosalyn began teaching at Hunter College, this time to returning veterans rather than classes of women. Aaron, who was then working at Montefiore Hospital in the Bronx, introduced her to Dr. Edith Quimby, a medical physicist who was studying the medical uses of radioactivity. This was an entirely new field, combining nuclear physics and medicine.

Of the 92 naturally-occurring kinds of elements that make up our universe (such as oxygen, hydrogen, carbon, silver, aluminum, etc.), many of the heavier one are naturally radioactive. The energy they give off can be tracked and measured by an instrument called a Geiger counter. In the 1920s and 1930s it was found that other elements could be made radioactive. This transformed the element into a slightly different form than its natural state. These various forms of the same element are called isotopes, and the radioactive ones are called radioisotopes. When the first nuclear reactor was built in 1942 (as part of the war effort), some of the byproducts were radioactive forms of certain elements. This led to the question,

Could they be used in medicine, to treat sick people? Some radioisotopes had become available to hospitals and research labs by the late 1940s.

Rosalyn Yalow was fascinated by the possibilities of the new field. She already had experience in building and using equipment for measuring radioactivity. She offered to work part-time in Dr. Quimby's lab to gain experience in the medical applications of radioactive elements. Dr. Quimby was instrumental in getting Rosalyn a position as a part-time consultant at the Bronx Veterans Administration Hospital. Besides treating patients who had been in the armed forces, this hospital also carried out medical research. The Veterans Administration decided that its hospitals needed radioisotope services to extend the new field of medicine.

Rosalyn was given a small laboratory in a converted janitor's closet. There she developed the hospital's radioisotope services, and carried out research projects with the staff physicians. She was still teaching full-time at Hunter, besides running her household, but her work at the hospital resulted in eight scientific publications. Partly because of her work, the VA set up similar services at other hospitals.

In 1950 Rosalyn left Hunter in order to devote herself fully to her work at the VA hospital. Her students were disappointed about her leaving; they enjoyed having a young enthusiastic teacher. But Rosalyn felt she could make more of a contribution to society by investigating possible uses of radioisotopes. For this purpose she needed a co-worker with medical training. Luckily she soon found such a person in Dr. Solomon Berson.

Sol Berson was a multi-talented young man who was completing his residency in internal medicine at the VA hospital. In July 1950 he and Rosalyn began their collaboration, which would continue for 22 years. Sol was a leader; outside of their lab, Rosalyn deferred to him. She let him give talks about their research, while she worked behind the scene, making travel arrangements and typing up his speeches. In the lab, however, they were equals. They enjoyed bouncing ideas off each other, and often both stayed in the lab late into the night. Like some married couples, they developed shortcuts in communicating with each other—no small talk, just basics concerning their work.

Rosalyn's dream of becoming a mother came true in the early 1950s. Benjamin Yalow was born in 1952. Although the hospital had a rule that pregnant women could not work past their fifth month of pregnancy, in Rosalyn's case this rule was ignored. A week after Ben's birth, she was back at work. Two years later, Elanna was born. The family had full-time help, but Rosalyn came home each day to eat lunch with the children. Sometimes she brought the children to the lab, where they passed the time playing with the guinea pigs that were kept for experimental purposes.

During this time, Rosalyn and Sol Berson were making important discoveries. They were interested in studying human hormones, and chose insulin because it was available in purified form and was fairly easy to work with. Insulin is important medically because millions of people are afflicted with the disease called diabetes. Individuals who are diabetic have high levels of sugar in the blood, presumably because the body does not produce enough insulin to break down the sugar and turn it into energy. Such patients were treated by injecting them with insulin from animals. Rosalyn also had a personal reason for working with insulin: her husband Aaron was diabetic.

To follow the path of insulin obtained from cattle in the human body, Rosalyn and Sol tagged it with radioactive iodine. Then they injected the tagged insulin into diabetes patients as well as healthy volunteers. Frequent blood samples were taken over several hours to see how fast the insulin disappeared. If there was something in the bodies of diabetics that attacked their insulin, then all traces of radioactive insulin would disappear rapidly from their bodies. But to their surprise, this did not happen. The insulin stayed longer in the bodies of the diabetics. Now Rosalyn and Sol had to figure out why. Could the diabetics be forming antibodies to counteract insulin?

Our bodies produce antibodies to fight off foreign substances. That is why we get certain diseases only once in our life. The first time our bodies form antibodies against the disease-carrying bacteria or virus, and this protects us from getting the disease again.

Rosalyn and Sol developed a procedure to measure precisely the amount of insulin in blood samples, using radiotagged insulin. Radioactive insulin and natural insulin compete equally in bonding with the antibody, which was obtained from guinea pigs. By measuring how much of the radioactive form bonded, the researchers could tell how much of the natural insulin was present. The technique compared test tubes containing known amounts of natural insulin, antibodies, and radiotagged insulin with test tubes containing an unknown amount of insulin and known amounts of antibodies and radiotagged insulin. The procedure became known as radioimmunoassay, or RIA for short.

The experiments showed that diabetics did indeed develop antibodies to the insulin they received, because their bodies recognized the insulin as a foreign substance. This was the first indication that a relatively simple substance like insulin could provoke an immunologic response.

The beauty of the technique was that it could be used for other substances, provided that the particular substance forms antibodies. The technique is so sensitive that it could detect a teaspoon of sugar in a lake 62 miles by 62 miles and thirty feet deep.

At first the scientific establishment hesitated to accept the findings, but Rosalyn was not discouraged. Publication of the two researchers' work came in 1956. Others soon confirmed their observations. Within a few years, the medical community adopted the RIA method to test for hundreds of substances. Whereas before, a cup of blood may have been required, now the same results could be obtained with only a few drops.

One application is a determination whether children that are very short for their age have too little of a growth hormone. Another application is the testing of newborn babies for a condition called hypothyroidism, in which the thyroid gland is not active enough. This condition leads to a stunted mental capacity. Thanks to the test, treatment can be started immediately on such infants.

The RIA method is also used to measure the amounts of illegal drugs in a person's bloodstream. Blood banks can screen blood donations to make sure they are free of drugs or viruses. Today there are close to sixty different RIA kits available to hospitals and labs.

Rosalyn and Sol made a good team. Each one learned from the other, and each felt free to criticize the other. "I had the good fortune" Rosalyn wrote "to learn medicine . . . directly from a master of physiology, anatomy, and clinical medicine." She had a logical mind, whereas Sol often had flashes of insight. They accomplished more working together than each one would have if working separately. They did not patent their discovery because they wanted it to benefit the whole world. "We made a scientific discovery and gave it to anyone who wanted to use it," Rosalyn said.

Their names were being mentioned as possible recipients of the Nobel Prize in Medicine and Physiology. But the years went by, and they were passed over time and again. In 1968 Sol Berson left to become department head at the Mount Sinai

School of Medicine, also in New York. Unfortunately, in 1972 he died of a heart attack, and thus lost his chance for a Nobel because only living scientists can be so honored. Many people thought that Rosalyn's chances for the Nobel were now very slim.

Rosalyn was devastated by Sol's untimely death. She requested that the laboratory where they had worked together for so many years be named The Solomon A. Berson Research Laboratory. In this way he will be remembered for his many contributions.

Rosalyn had enough drive and self-confidence to continue her research without Sol's input. She acquired a new research partner, a young physician named Eugene Straus. Then early one morning in the fall of 1977, she got a phone call from Stockholm. The caller, Professor Luft, head of a Nobel committee, said she had won half of that year's prize in physiology and medicine. The other half would be shared by Dr. Andrew V. Schally and Dr. Roger Guillemin, who had used the RIA technique to make important discoveries about hormones in the brain. Suddenly Rosalyn's life changed.

The news spread immediately. At her husband's suggestion, she went to change her clothes. "As soon as they hear what's happened, the photographers and reporters will descend on you," Aaron told her. Soon her office filled with people. Aaron and Ben arrived to participate in a hastily arranged party in the lab. Rosalyn told reporters she was thankful for the thirty years of support of her work by the Veterans Administration. She was of course sad that Sol Berson had not lived long enough to share this honor with her.

The weeks until December, when the prizes were awarded, were busy ones. She wrote several research papers, and gave talks she had scheduled. She realized she needed new clothes. A leading fashion designer designed a blue chiffon dress and brocade vest to wear at the award ceremony. Before leaving for Sweden, Rosalyn and Aaron flew to California to attend their daughter Elanna's wedding. The newly-weds decided to spend part of their honeymoon in Sweden so that they could see Rosalyn get her award.

In Sweden, there were nonstop events for the honored guests—dinners, cocktail parties, and interviews. The award ceremony itself drew 1800 people. The next day was taken up by lectures given by each winner. In hers, Rosalyn reported on new work she had recently completed. She gave credit to Sol Berson for his part.

Since she was the first American-trained woman to win in any of the sciences, Rosalyn Yalow was now a celebrity. Newspapers reported everything she said in public. She enjoyed the attention. But as before, she put in eighty to one hundred hours a week in the lab. The excitement of perhaps discovering new secrets was still with her.

A few years later, Rosalyn and her staff moved to new, more spacious quarters. Apart from the main laboratories, Rosalyn had her own suite of offices, and rooms containing rabbits, guinea pigs, and mice that are used for various experiments. On weekends, she came in herself to care for the animals, nuzzling each one and talking to them tenderly as she handled them.

Doctors from other countries came to work on special projects there. Rosalyn called them her "professional children"; she encouraged them and offered advice when it was needed. To students, she always said "Do what you enjoy doing most. Set goals for yourself and then live up to them."

Many other awards came to Rosalyn. In 1976 she received the prestigious Albert Lasker Prize for Basic Medical Research. She became a member of the National Academy of Sciences. She was named winner of the Eli Lilly Award of the American Diabetes Association, and received the National

Medal of Science in 1988. But when she was nominated in 1978 for the Ladies' Home Journal Woman of the Year Award, she refused it, saying she did not believe in prizes for women only. She felt women should have an equal chance with men to win awards, no more and no less. Her outspokenness and occasional self-righteous manner made her unpopular among scientists.

As a celebrity, Rosalyn found that anything she wrote or said became instant news. One of the issues she spoke out about was the public's fear of low-level radiation. Radioactive laboratory waste has such a low level of radiation that it does not present a health hazard, she maintained. Radiation is encountered everywhere: it bombards the earth and everything on it from outer space. Therefore our bodies all contain a tiny amount of radioactivity. It apparently does not cause cancer, as some people believe, since mountainous areas where radiation is higher have no more cases of cancer than other areas.

Rosalyn also believes that all high school students should have at least one year's study of general science. This will make them better citizens later on, when they are old enough to vote on matters involving pollution, for example.

Rosalyn was always curious and enthusiastic

about her chosen field. "I'll never retire," she said in the early 1980s, "even though there are other things I'd like to try."

On New Year's Day 1995 Rosalyn suffered a stroke. But two years later, when fully recovered, she was back in her lab, although not putting in one hundred hours a week as she used to do. She truly loved being on the trail of new knowledge.

"As long as you're learning you're not old," she liked to say. That was the attitude that propelled the young girl reading on a Bronx rooftop to celebrity status as a leading scientist, recognized by the whole world for her achievements.

Dorothy Hodgkin

Dorothy Crowfoot, at eleven, was entranced by the pretty blue crystals formed by her classmates' experiment in their science class. Always curious about the materials that make up things around us, she already knew that salt and sugar are crystals. At the Leman School in England, she learned that crystals, besides occurring naturally, can be grown. This interest would guide Dorothy throughout her adult life. Her persistence and determination to carry out difficult investigations, in spite of being limited by a crippling disease, made crystallography an essential scientific tool. Her work led eventually to the widespread use of penicillin and other antibiotics.

Dorothy was born on May 12, 1910, in Cairo, Egypt, which was then a British colony. Her father John Crowfoot was a British administrator who supervised Egyptian schools and ancient monuments, and was interested in digging up remains of ancient civilizations. Her mother Molly collected plants, and passed this interest on to Dorothy and her three other daughters.

When World War I began in 1914, the Crowfoot family was in England. The parents returned to Egypt, where the government needed John, but without their children; England was considered a safer place for them. For the next four years, the Crowfoot children lived with a nanny in a house close to their grandmother's home. During this four-year period, they saw their mother only once. When the war ended, Molly returned to her children, and later that year John came back to England too. In the years that followed, the family spent their summers together; after three months in England, John returned to his post abroad, and Molly followed three months later. These long periods of separation from her parents made Dorothy self-reliant and independent.

At school, Dorothy especially enjoyed her chemistry class. She set up a small laboratory at home so that she could do experiments outside of school. One of the first experiments was growing crystals of copper sulfate, the blue crystals she had admired so much in class. She had learned that a crystal is made up of atoms arranged in a repeating pattern, and each kind of crystal has a characteristic shape. Some are box-like, some are pyramids, some are lacy like snowflakes. They can be any size – up to several thousand pounds. If the crystalline substance is quite pure, the crystals are perfect in shape; if impurities are present, this interferes with the structure, and the crystals have irregular shapes.

During a six-month stay with her parents in the African country of Sudan, Dorothy learned how to prospect for gold. Putting this new skill into practice in her parents' yard, she found a shiny black mineral. A family friend helped her identify it chemically as a mixture of iron and titanium called ilmenite.

At fourteen, Dorothy was an attractive girl with blonde curly hair, shy and usually wrapped up in her own thoughts. Overcoming her shyness, she participated in her school's mock election by representing the Labor Party. This experience gave her a liking for political debate, which was further reinforced by attending with her mother a meeting of the League of Nations (forerunner of the United Nations) in Geneva, Switzerland.

By the time Dorothy graduated from high school, she had decided to study chemistry at Oxford University. But then she discovered she was unprepared for the entrance examination. She had not studied Latin or a second science, both of which were required. Her mother tutored her in botany, and she managed to learn enough Latin to pass the exam. She then took a six-month vacation to Jerusalem, where her father was excavating early Christian churches. Dorothy was given the job of copying mosaic designs on the floors of the churches. She enjoyed her summer there, and for a brief time considered studying archeology rather than chemistry. In both fields "you're finding what's there and then trying to make sense of what you find."

In 1928 Dorothy began her studies at Oxford — one of a small number of women students there. She listened avidly to lectures that explained how X-rays could be used to "see" inside molecules. Molecules are basic substances made up of atoms bound together in a certain way. Some molecules contain a small number of atoms and are simple in structure, while others are huge and complex. X-rays can bounce off the atoms of a substance, just like light is reflected from a network of solid masses separated by empty spaces. The angles of reflection can amplify or diminish the intensity of the light or the X-rays. This so-called diffraction shows where there are solids and where there are spaces. From the pattern of spots recorded on photographic film, and their darkness or lightness, one can learn about the structure of the molecules making up a crystal. A series of mathematical calculations are required to interpret the spots on the film. This technique was first discovered in 1912 by the British scientist William Bragg.

Oxford separated its women students from the men students, allegedly so as not to distract the men. Women had to follow certain rules, such as getting permission to visit a male student's apartment and taking along a chaperone. It was big news when the women's college of Oxford first allowed men to attend their Sunday afternoon teas. But the strict social rules did not bother Dorothy. She concentrated on her studies. Later on, she began to join friends at tea parties or the theater. Friends recognized that although Dorothy was a quiet person, she could be interesting to talk to since she had done so many unusual things.

After three years at Oxford, Dorothy decided on research as her career goal. A fourth year would involve doing original research. She planned to specialize in X-ray crystallography, and was given lab space in the university museum. Her research progressed well, although the math part was tedious. At the end of the fourth year, Dorothy achieved what Oxford called a first-class degree in chemistry—only the third woman to earn it at

Oxford. She then moved to the University of Cambridge, where she was offered an opportunity to work with John D. Bernal, a well-known scientist, who was using X-ray crystallography on large biological molecules.

Bernal was a brilliant researcher with radical political views. He had joined the Communist party in England in his belief that science should be applied for the betterment of mankind. He encouraged women to work in his lab. Dorothy enjoyed the informal atmosphere that prevailed among his workers. Under Bernal's direction, Dorothy investigated various kinds of crystals of biological interest. She regarded Bernal's collection of crystals, sent to him from all over, as "gold just lying around waiting to be picked up."

Bernal's style was to publish a short report on a particular crystal and then move on to others. Dorothy's name was on twelve such papers as co-author. One of these was the first to show an X-ray photo of a protein (one of the group of substances that carry out processes in a living body.) Dorothy and Bernal showed that the secret of photographing proteins lay in keeping the crystals wet.

After a year, Oxford offered Dorothy a research position that would include some teaching. But she liked Cambridge better; it had more facilities, and she really did not want to teach. Oxford then came up with another offer: she could stay another year with Bernal; after that, Oxford would pay her a salary to support her research, and give her the title Official Fellow and Tutor in Natural Science. She accepted this offer, feeling it would help her career.

Her lab was again in the basement of the University's museum, near displays of dinosaur bones and dead insects. It was a rather ghostly atmosphere for an up-to-date laboratory. The single window was high above the floor, with a platform just below it, reachable by a circular stairway. There Dorothy kept her microscope where she studied her precious crystals. Next door was the X-ray room, with a large table where she and her students could analyze their data. Realizing she needed more modern equipment, she wheedled enough money out of a chemical company for the purchases.

She continued work begun with Bernal, concentrating on cholesterol, an important substance in animal tissues. Whereas others had determined the relative amounts of carbon, hydrogen, and oxygen in the cholesterol molecule, no one knew how they were arranged three-dimensionally. The X-ray investigation would require an aptitude for math, attention to detail, and a good imagination. Dorothy showed she had all these attributes. Inserting a heavy atom such as iodine into the cholesterol molecule helped considerably in interpreting the data. Dorothy's calculations produced an "electron density map" of a crystal, which looked like a map of a mountainous country. The peaks of the mountains corresponded to the highest electron density, and therefore the most likely places for the atoms. Dorothy became expert at interpreting such electron density maps. Soon she had determined the spatial arrangement of atoms in cholesterol.

Another substance that found its way to Dorothy's lab was insulin. She was eager to be the first to take X-ray photos of it. After trying various procedures, she obtained a lovely photo. "The moment when I developed the photograph and saw the central pattern of minute reflections was probably the most exciting of my life" she wrote. A description of this work was published in April 1935 – the first paper to carry her name alone. It established Dorothy, at not quite 25, as an original scientist. She gained a reputation of having remarkable insight about X-ray photos.

In the mid 1930s, a pain in her hands led Dorothy to consult a doctor. The diagnosis was rheumatoid arthritis, an incurable disease caused by the body's attack on its own tissues. Dorothy's feet and hands became increasingly crippled, but she never complained of the pain, and she never let it interfere with her work.

Oxford's custom of keeping its women chemists isolated from the all-male chemistry club bothered Dorothy a great deal. However, she succeeded in developing an active social life. In 1937 she met Thomas Hodgkin, who came from a family of historians, doctors, and scientists. He and Dorothy found they had much in common, and so they got married in December 1937. In the years that followed, two boys and a girl were born. Help with the children was readily available, so Dorothy continued to work. Also, Thomas realized she was the more creative of the two, and deserved the opportunity to continue her research. Two older women helped out at home. Dorothy went home to have lunch with the children each day, and returned in time for dinner later.

After finishing her work on cholesterol, Dorothy turned to penicillin. By 1940, England was at war, and penicillin was badly needed to treat war injuries. If its structure was known, perhaps it could be produced in large quantities. But penicillin proved to be far more difficult to analyze than cholesterol. What the researchers did not know was that penicillin crystals came in several shapes; it turned out that American and British scientists were working with four different types.

Equipment was in short supply and budgets were tight. When Bernal went into war research, he gave his equipment to Dorothy. Halfway through the war, she got access to an early IBM computer, which accelerated the work. In 1946, after four years with penicillin, Dorothy wrote "It was a nice day when we could set up the model first precisely in three dimensions, and rang up our friends to come and see what penicillin actually was." Bernal's reaction was, "You will get the Nobel Prize for this." She replied, "I would far rather be elected a Fellow of the Royal Society." In time she would have both.

After the war, drug companies used Dorothy's model to develop a number of varieties of penicillin, tailor-made to attack certain bacteria. These drugs, called collectively antibiotics, have revolutionized the treatment of diseases.

As Dorothy and other scientists began explaining the structure of crystals, others used this information to examine what can be done with impure crystals. This led to the development of transistors—small electronic devices that are now used in television sets, computers, and communication satellites.

Whereas Dorothy's reputation on the international scene was assured, Oxford with its red tape of boards and committees still did not give her an official appointment in either the chemistry or the mineralogy department. Her salary as a College Fellow barely covered her living expenses, because Thomas maintained a separate home in northern England, where he was working. Male College Fellows held also University appointments, and thus in effect earned two salaries. In May 1945, Dorothy was finally given a University appointment with the title University Demonstrator in Chemical Crystallography. Thomas was named director of Oxford's adult education center, so for a time the family was reunited. In 1947 Dorothy was elected to the Royal Society of London, England's most prestigious scientific organization—only the third woman in its 287-year history.

After a trip to the U.S., where many universities invited her to speak about her work on penicillin, it was Thomas' turn to travel. He was invited to various African countries to advise them on setting up adult education systems. In that capacity he became friends with many in the independence movements of countries that had been British colonies, who later became leaders in their respective countries.

With Thomas spending increasing amounts of time in Africa, Dorothy rented a large house so that her sister Joan and Joan's four children could live with her. Dorothy's two youngest still lived at home. Six youngsters made for an unruly household, that frequently included overnight guests also. Leaving Joan in charge, this arrangement allowed Dorothy to visit her husband in Africa periodically.

Dorothy's research attracted a number of women students. One was Margaret Thatcher, who went on to become England's Prime Minister in 1979. She and Thomas often argued about politics over dinner. Dorothy limited her team to ten students. They were known as Dorothy's Cats, and Dorothy was the "Mother Cat", who enjoyed mothering her students. Unlike the British practice of calling everyone by their last name, in Dorothy's lab only first names were used.

Because of her work with penicillin, Dorothy was well-known in the drug industry. In 1948 she was given some red crystals of vitamin B12, the vitamin that allows the human body to make red blood cells and thereby protects it against anemia. It has a complicated structure. The fact that it contains a cobalt atom sparked Dorothy's enthusiasm for the new project, because that would make the data somewhat easier to interpret.

For six years Dorothy and her team worked on vitamin B12. Her intuition and confidence were legendary by this time. Her instinct was "the product of her phenomenal knowledge of the relevant chemistry and physics, her long experience, and her marvelous memory for detail", according to one student. Her hunches usually proved to be right.

In another respect, the B12 project was easier for Dorothy than previous ones. An American, Kenneth Trueblood, visiting Oxford in 1953, offered Dorothy the use of an early computer on the University of California's Los Angeles campus. Accordingly, six years of data were mailed to California, and Trueblood mailed back his results. Dorothy was ecstatic over the results that came back. The computer could do in hours what had taken weeks before. In 1956—eight years after starting—Dorothy announced the structural formula of vitamin B12. William Bragg, the inventor of X-ray crystallography, cheered her announcement: "Nothing short of magnificent — absolutely thrilling!"

In the post-war years, Dorothy's career and her

political beliefs clashed. She was instrumental in organizing the International Union of Crystallography. The group wanted to include everyone in the field, regardless of their nationality. But the U.S. refused to let eastern Europeans and Russians enter the country. This was the period of the "Cold War", when anyone with any connection to a Communist country or Communism was unwelcome. Dorothy herself was excluded from a meeting in the U.S. because she had once joined an organization that included Communists.

By the late 1950s, Dorothy's name was being mentioned as a possible Nobel Prize winner. She was recognized as the supreme crystallographer. After having been nominated several times, she was finally named the winner in chemistry in 1964. She was in Ghana with Thomas when the announcement reached her. Of course she was elated! All the years of diligent, sometimes discouraging, work was being recognized. Thomas' department of African studies celebrated with an enormous party, complete with native dancers. It was probably the most unusual Nobel celebration party ever.

Two of Dorothy's children, now grown with careers of their own, came to Stockholm for the award ceremony: Toby from India, and Liz from

Zambia, Africa. Luke, the oldest, was working in Algeria and could not leave. Two of Dorothy's sisters came also.

Dorothy's citation read "for her determination by X-ray techniques of the structure of important biochemical substances, especially penicillin and vitamin B12 . . . the crowning triumph of X-ray crystallographic analysis." As was the custom, in her speech she thanked all the people who had worked with her or encouraged her over the years. Her only regret was that Bernal, her main source of inspiration, did not share the award.

Back at Oxford, Dorothy undertook another major project. For a long time she had wanted to get back to investigating insulin, the hormone whose lack causes diabetes. It took her team until 1969 to work out how the 777 atoms making up insulin are put together. This break-through led to further research in treating patients with diabetes. By this time X-ray crystallography was often the only method of discovering the three-dimensional shape of a large molecule. It was faster and more accurate than the old method of chemical degradation.

After the Nobel, the next honor for Dorothy was the Order of Merit, bestowed by England's Queen Elizabeth II. At the ensuing banquet, she sat next to the artist Henry Moore. He was so impressed at the sight of her twisted hands that he asked to draw them. The drawing now hangs in the Royal Society building beside Dorothy's official portrait.

The fame that came with a Nobel Prize allowed Dorothy to speak out on issues beyond science. During the 1960s and 1970s she campaigned tirelessly for peace organizations. At Dorothy's urging, Margaret Thatcher, then prime minister, visited the Soviet Union to improve relations between the two countries. This helped her win re-election in 1987.

"How to abolish arms and achieve a peaceful world is necessarily our first objective," Dorothy wrote in 1981 ". . . if some—and preferably all—of the million dollars spent every minute on arms were turned to the abolition of poverty from the world, many causes of conflict would vanish."

After her retirement from Oxford in 1977, Dorothy was very busy traveling and giving speeches. Her hair had turned from golden blonde to white, but she still had plenty of stamina and enthusiasm for her topic. She felt that international relations could best be advanced by face-to-face dialogue. In this pursuit, she traveled thousands of miles and met many world leaders. Her efforts led to her election as president of the International Union of Crystallography from 1972-75, and of the

Pugwash Conference on Science and World Affairs (a group of scientists devoted to finding ways to prevent wars) from 1975 to 1988.

Dorothy was instrumental in forging links with Chinese scientists, at a time when they were not allowed to publish their work outside of China. Within a few years, regular exchanges were set up between Chinese and British scientists. Researchers who came from India to gain experience in Dorothy's lab gave her connections to that country too. In India, as in China, she made the scientists feel that they had a special relationship with her.

In 1993 Dorothy traveled to China for a conference, in spite of being confined to a wheelchair and needing 24-hour nursing care. Surrounded by scientific friends, she perked up; they, on the other hand, were saddened to see her so frail and immobile. The following year, she broke her hip a second time, and two weeks later she died.

At her memorial service, a long-time friend stated, "Dorothy will be remembered as a great chemist, a saintly, tolerant, and gentle lover of people, and a devoted protagonist of peace."

Mary Leakey

Twelve-year-old Mary Nicol gazed in wonder at the animals painted on the walls of a cave. In the dim light, the horses and bison seemed to come alive. Mary wondered about the kind of people that had made the paintings.

She was in southern France, where her father Erskine Nicol had brought his family from their native England. A friend of the family had taken Mary and her mother to see the cave paintings. When Mary's father was not busy painting landscapes, he often took Mary to a cave where another friend was digging to find ancient stone tools. Mary helped sift through buckets of dirt that were brought out. She learned to recognize flint blades and scrapers—stones that had been shaped by the hands of early humans. Here she discovered the joys of collecting.

The family's idyllic life came to an end when Mr. Nicol fell ill and died in the spring of 1926, when Mary was thirteen. Mary and her mother returned to England, and Mary was enrolled in a convent school. Up to that time her only teachers had been her father and a tutor. Mary was miserable at the school; she hated sitting in classes to learn subjects that did not interest her, and she felt she had nothing in common with the other students. After causing a small explosion in a chemistry class, she was expelled. Soon thereafter, her formal schooling came to an end.

On her own, Mary kept up her interest in archeology, the study of prehistoric ancestors of man as revealed by their artifacts. At seventeen, she discovered she could attend classes at University College in London, even though not formally admitted as a student. This was a turning point in her life. No more a rebellious teenager, she saw that in archeology she could perhaps do something important. She wrote letters to various archeologists asking to join their team of workers.

One letter resulted in her being offered a position helping Dorothy Liddell, who was excavating a prehistoric site in southwest England. As part of Dr. Liddell's team, Mary unearthed pottery and other items. "Dorothy was an enormous help in training me, showing me how to dig properly, and making it quite clear that females could go to the top," Mary wrote later.

During her three summers with Dr. Liddell, Mary made sketches of the flint tools they found. Her drawings were published along with Dr. Liddell's descriptions. They caught the eye of another archeologist, Dr. Gertrude Caton-Thompson, who asked Mary to draw stone tools found by her team in Egypt. Pleased with Mary's work, she invited Mary to a lecture at the Royal Anthropological Institute in London. The speaker was Louis Leakey, who had made interesting discoveries in Kenya, Africa. Louis, ten years older than Mary, was already a well-known archeologist.

At a dinner following the lecture, Mary managed to sit next to Louis. She was pleased that he treated her with respect, like an equal. They discovered that they shared a love of animals and of travel to wild places. Louis asked Mary to illustrate his upcoming book titled "Adam's Ancestors."

The two kept in touch through letters and visits. Mary realized she was falling in love with a married man, although Louis' marriage was already failing. In October 1934 Louis returned to Africa, after asking Mary to join him there. Mary's mother wanted her to forget about Louis, but she agreed to accompany Mary to South Africa and Zimbabwe to visit prehistoric sites. After they had viewed early rock paintings, Mary, ignoring her mother's wishes, took a plane to Tanzania, where Louis was to meet her. Mrs. Nicol had to return to England alone.

Mary and Louis drove to Olduvai Gorge, where Louis was supervising a dig. Olduvai is a dry, hot, dusty place, where lions, giraffes, and rhinoceros are common. In the soil, human remains are mixed in with remains of pigs and antelopes.

Finding fossils is slow work, requiring patience and persistence. Records and drawings must be kept showing the position of every find and its surroundings. Trenches must be dug to determine the geological age of each layer. To make sure nothing is missed, all the soil in a given area, usually about a square yard, is put through a sieve.

The deepest layer at Olduvai was dated at two million years. Because bones and tools were found together, this was considered evidence that the animals were eaten by hominids—the term used for early humans and near-humans.

Mary was excited when she found two pieces of a human skull. Her skill and quiet ways won over the native diggers, who at first resented her presence.

Louis and Mary returned to England, and when Louis' divorce was final, they were married. In January 1937 they returned to Africa. Louis had a grant to support him during a study of the customs and traditions of the Kikuyu tribe. While he worked on this, Mary began an excavation nearby, where she unearthed many tools and pottery pieces. These were packed into boxes and shipped to England for further study. She and Louis divided the work to be done each evening: she catalogued the stones, while he worked on the bones.

During World War II, Louis was hired by the British government as an intelligence agent. He also became the curator of a museum in Nairobi, the capital of Kenya. When Kenya's northern neighbor Ethiopia was taken over by Italy in 1937, the British feared that Italy would close the Suez Canal, thereby shutting off Britain's oil supply. Louis was pressed into service to help send weapons and supplies to Ethiopian guerilla fighters. As a handwriting expert, he was also asked to sort through piles of hand-written documents.

All this left Louis little time for excavating. But Mary continued to dig energetically, stopping only long enough to give birth to their first child, a son named Jonathan, on November 4, 1940. Although she liked having a child, Mary wrote, "I have no intention of allowing motherhood to disrupt my work as an archeologist."

Whenever Louis could get away, he, Mary, the baby, their Dalmatian dogs, and any number of friends headed out on collecting trips. One of these took them to Olorgesailie, the site of a dried-up lake about forty miles south of Nairobi. The group fanned out, all eyes on the ground. Soon shouts arose: "Look what I found!" Several layers of implements were uncovered. Mary returned many times to this site, but could not connect the various layers with any time frame. Later scientists dated the oldest layer at 900,000 years.

A baby girl born to the Leakeys in January 1943 died of dysentery when only three months old. Both parents were deeply hurt by the loss. Then in December 1944, a second son, Richard, was born. A third son named Phillip would be born later.

In March 1946 Mary and her two children sailed to England because Mary's mother was ill. Mrs. Nicol passed away two weeks after their arrival. Louis was busy planning a Pan-African Congress of Prehistory and Paleontology, which was shaping up as a very important conference. Louis joined Mary in England, partly to promote the upcoming conference. He brought with him an ape-like jaw he had excavated, of a species that was given the name Proconsul. He showed it to everyone he met, even on a British television show. Other scientists criticized Louis because he had a habit of announcing discoveries in newspapers and popular magazines rather than in scholarly journals.

The conference took place in Nairobi in January

1937. Mary led the visitors on a tour of several sites she had worked on. She was not as accustomed as Louis to speaking in public, but her enthusiasm was evident in speaking about her discoveries. This conference established Mary as a scientist in her own right, whereas before, many thought that she just tagged along with Louis. Several of the sixty visiting scientists were impressed enough to help the Leakeys gain funding for their latest project. With their new-found money, they purchased a truck which they converted into a mobile home.

Mary's main interest now was to find remains of apes from which "we might hope to find some evidence of man's own line of evolution." In September 1948 she thought she had found what she was searching for. Walking through a gully on Rusinga, an island in Lake Victoria, she noticed a tooth exposed on a slope. She shouted for Louis to come. They brushed away the dirt carefully to reveal the greater part of a skull and jawbone. It was unmistakably a skull of Proconsul—"a wildly exciting find", Mary wrote. Louis decided that Mary should take it to England. When her plane landed in London, Proconsul was already front-page news. The press proclaimed Mary a first-class scientist. Close study of the skull led to the conclusion that it belonged to a common ancestor of both humans and apes.

Another exciting find came in July 1959 at Olduvai. Louis lay ill in bed, while Mary was out exploring. A jawbone sticking out of the ground caught her eye. She dashed back to camp. "I've got him, I've got him," she shouted, "the one we've been looking for!" Louis jumped out of bed and accompanied Mary back to the site. They looked at each other with joy: they had discovered the world's earliest known human.

Louis named it *Zinjanthropus boisei* (*Zinjanthropus* meaning man from East Africa and boisei in honor of Charles Boise, who had supported their work with several grants.) Louis estimated its age as between 600,000 and one million years, and described it as "connecting the link between South African near-men and true man as we know him." Later studies dated the skull at 1.75 million years.

Louis' time at Olduvai was limited, so he made Mary director of the excavations. She insisted on hiring her own native workers. While her team worked, she wanted quiet; no singing or talking, so they could concentrate on what they were doing. This stern manner astonished the natives; they were not used to seeing a woman in charge. "Kali mzungu" they called her—"prickly white person." While Mary worked, a cigarette usually dangled from her lips. Her Dalmatian dogs were always close at hand.

Mary's excavations showed that early hominids seemed to use certain sites for eating and sleeping. Mary pictured them gathered in one spot to eat meat from animals they had hunted, using sharp stone flakes to cut meat from the bones, and hammer stones to crush bones to get at the marrow. In an adjacent area were ribs, jawbones, and vertebrae—bones that do not contain marrow. Mary believed that the hominids had tossed those bones away, probably over bushes.

Work began at seven a.m. after breakfast, and continued until one. Then everyone returned to camp for lunch. Fossils and tools were sorted until 5:30. Mary and any visiting scientists or friends dressed up for dinner, which was preceded by a cocktail hour. Conversation was the only activity until bedtime.

Sometimes the roaring of lions and snorting of leopards kept everyone awake. When the leopards seemed to be close to the camp, Mary stood outside her hut and banged on a pot to frighten them off. Once hyenas broke into the refrigerator and made off with most of the meat supply. Mary got up and threw a firecracker at them.

Louis started supervising a new dig. This annoyed Mary, who felt it was taking money and manpower away from her dig at Olduvai. But in 1961 and 1962, new bones of pre-humans were found at Louis' site, covering the time frame 1.8 million to 800,000 years ago. These were eventually named *Homo habilis*, meaning handy man—the first tool maker. The definition of being human was now re-defined: walking upright, erect posture, hands that could grip, and a brain capacity of at least 600 cubic centimeters. (This was later modified when it was discovered that chimpanzees also use tools.)

By 1964 the Leakeys were famous, but the years ahead would not be happy ones for them as a couple. Louis spread himself too thin. Mary's method of working was to stick to one project and see it through. Louis rushed from one project to another. This often made Mary feel as though she was left behind to look after details. Louis spent increasing time overseas giving fund-raising speeches. He spent money as soon as it came in, while Mary was barely getting by. She thought some of his new projects were a waste of time. Being much more cautious than Louis in arriving at conclusions, she criticized his new ideas. But many of his ideas about finding missing links in Africa had proven to be right.

In early 1968 the University of Witwatersrand in South Africa announced it would award honorary doctor's degrees to both Louis and Mary Leakey. This gave Mary a great measure of self-confidence. Whereas before, in any discussion of stones and bones, she would say "We'll have to ask Louis about that," now she did not hesitate to state her own interpretations. Olduvai had become her own project; she no longer needed Louis there. More and more, they grew apart and led separate lives.

Mary tried in vain to get Louis to cut back on his work. In London for another lecture tour, Louis suffered a fatal heart attack on October 1, 1972. His body was flown back to Kenya for burial. A few days after the funeral, Mary was back at Olduvai excavating new layers.

She had become more judgmental of other people, measuring them according to her own demanding standards. It was easy to fall out of favor with Mary. She chose who may visit her at Olduvai, and how long they may stay. "Above all, I wanted to be left in peace to get on with my work," she wrote. Anyone who rubbed her the wrong way or annoyed her in some manner was banished from her camp.

She could not, however, banish tourists. Olduvai, situated near safari lodges and herds of wildlife, became a regular stopping place for tourists. Louis had always welcomed them, but Mary considered them a nuisance. In 1973 alone, over 20,000 tourists came. Mostly in self-defense, Mary built a small museum near the gorge, with pamphlets and postcards for tourists, hoping this would satisfy their curiosity.

She had described *Homo habilis*, the earliest toolmakers, and their older cousins *Australopithecus boisei* (the previously-named *Zinjanthropus*.) Now she wanted to do the same for *Homo erectus*, who was thought to have appeared on the scene in Africa about 1.4 million years ago. A question that needed to be resolved was: Could *Homo erectus* and *Homo habilis* have lived side by side, perhaps as long as a million years? Mary was never able to prove this.

In the spring of 1974, a neighbor showed Mary some fossils that had come from an area called Laetoli, an hour's drive from Olduvai. Mary put her team to work there. In short order they unearthed fossil remains of thirteen hominids. Mary thought they must be older than those from Olduvai. Since the tools of Olduvai were two million years old and showed much variety, Mary felt that human ancestors must have been making stone tools even earlier. But how much earlier? She was excited when dating analysis showed the fossils were 3.35 to 3.75 million years old.

She flew to America to announce her new finds at the National Geographic Society in Washington, D.C. From the Society she received a grant of $40,000. After collecting a gold medal from the American Society of Women Geographers, and garnering headlines in all newspapers, Mary returned to Olduvai.

At Laetoli, Mary's team then found a series of footprints that looked like they were made by a human. This proved that hominids walked upright as long as 3.65 million years ago, the age of the surrounding volcanic ash. This was much earlier than was previously thought. In addition, they found a lower jaw that led to a major controversy.

Donald Johanson, an archeologist working in Ethiopia, had unearthed a hominid skeleton that was given the name *Australopithecus afarensis*, or more familiarly, Lucy. Johanson considered Lucy to be the same species as Mary's bones from Laetoli. Mary did not agree.

Johanson was ambitious, and hoped to outdo any of the Leakeys, or least become as famous. He had visited Mary at Olduvai, and the two had got along well. Mary had told him, "You're like a Leakey; you can find fossils." He appreciated her words of praise.

In May 1978, both Mary and Johanson were in Stockholm, Sweden, for a scientific meeting. Mary was to receive the Golden Linnaean Medal from the king of Sweden in recognition of her work. Johanson was among the first to speak; he devoted much of his speech to Mary's Laetoli finds. This made Mary furious. She was the next speaker; but everything she planned to say had already been said by Johanson. She would look like a fool if she simply repeated that information. This led to a rift between the two.

Johanson chose one of Mary's fossils as the prototype—a reference specimen against which others would be compared. But Mary's specimen differed from Johanson's in both time and space. The name was bound to cause confusion, pointing to one site, while the prototype's origin pointed to another. Mary insisted that her name be omitted from Johanson's upcoming publication, because she did not agree with his conclusions. The issue of whether one or two species are involved is still not cleared up.

More footprints were found at Laetoli, two parallel prints, distinctly human, preserved in volcanic ash. Though usually unemotional, Mary exclaimed, "Now this is really something to put on the mantelpiece!" But why was one set so much larger than the other? The mystery was solved by a wildlife photographer named Alan Root. He explained the larger prints were actually made by two individuals, one behind the other, with the second one walking in the footsteps of the first. It could have been a family; a male followed closely by a female, with a juvenile walking beside them.

Mary's satisfaction with her recent successes was tempered with worry about her son Richard. His kidneys were about to fail. He had carved out a career of his own in archeology and paleontology, and refused to slow down. His brother Phillip offered him one of his own kidneys. The operation was a success, and Richard felt he was reborn.

In 1983 Mary retired from field work. Her work at Olduvai had spanned fifty years. She had "weathered floods, droughts, prowling lions, invasions of vipers, grasshoppers, tourists, and students; ash falls from volcanic Mount Lengai; drunken cooks and mischievous Masai (natives)..." She returned to the house near Nairobi that she and Louis had built. Her analysis of items from Olduvai's upper layer was almost complete, and would become the fifth volume on findings at

Olduvai Gorge. She also worked on an autobiography, and enjoyed the company of friends, her children and grandchildren. Several universities conferred honorary degrees on her.

Stephen Jay Gould, a well-known zoologist, called Mary Leakey "the unsung hero" of the search for human origins. Twice she had discovered the earliest humans — *Australopithecus boisei,* and *Australopithecus afarensis* from Laetoli. She is credited with finding the oldest evidence of the upright mode of walking.

A shopkeeper in London once asked Mary, after seeing her name on a check she had just written, "Are you the prehistoric Mrs. Leakey?" Mary laughingly replied, "I suppose so." When she died on December 9, 1996, in Nairobi, her scientific reputation had surpassed that of her husband.

Rosalind Franklin

Some scientists work methodically and cautiously, always looking for false reasoning or wrong interpretations. Others work by speculation, depending on wild ideas, flashes of insight, and intuition to explain certain observations. Rosalind Franklin was the first kind of scientist. Her training made her cautious and questioning. This aspect of her personality may have cost her a place among the leading scientists of the 20th century. Yet her contributions should not be minimized.

Rosalind was born on July 20, 1920, the second of five children in a well-to-do English Jewish family. Her father Ellis Franklin was a banker who also devoted much energy to public service. Family vacations were spent at the seashore or in travel abroad, and the children were cared for by nannies. Rosalind's intelligence was evident at an early age. An aunt wrote of six-year-old Rosalind that she is "alarmingly clever—she spends all her time doing arithmetic for pleasure." She was curious about everything, and asked numerous questions. She liked making things—sewing, drawing, and woodworking.

At eight she was sent to a seaside boarding school for health reasons, after suffering through many colds and bouts of flu. While she would have preferred living at home, she threw herself into her studies, as well as sports and handiwork such as knitting. Every week the pupils were ranked; Rosalind strove to be first in her class, and achieved it fairly often.

At eleven, Rosalind entered St. Paul's, a London day school known for its academic rigor and its philosophy that every girl should be prepared for a career. Rosalind won a scholarship throughout her years at St. Paul's. Playing on the school's hockey, cricket, and tennis teams gave her a lifelong love of sports. A love of hiking had already been instilled by her parents.

By the time she was fifteen, Rosalind knew she wanted to be a scientist. She loved the logic and clear-cut answers that science presented. Mr. Franklin, like many fathers at that time, thought higher education made women unhappy. But seeing Rosalind's determination, he allowed her to go to college. A college education for a girl was something only wealthy families could afford; in most English families boys had priority.

After passing the entrance exam and spending the summer of 1938 in France, Rosalind entered Newnham College, a branch of Cambridge University. Her courses included chemistry, physics, math, mineralogy, and scientific German. Long hours spent in the college laboratories kept her from forming close friendships. Cambridge did not award degrees to its women students at that time, but the five hundred or so young women who were admitted as students considered themselves fortunate.

War between England and Germany seemed inevitable as the months of 1939 went by. As England prepared itself by building bomb shelters in London, life in Cambridge, fifty miles away, went on as usual. During Rosalind's second year, however, air raid warnings frequently interrupted the students' sleep or study time. At the signal, all students were expected to hurry down into the trenches that had been dug. Rosalind resented these interruptions; once she and two others ignored the warning signal, and were severely scolded. Several years later, Rosalind, wanting to do something for the war effort, became an air raid warden and helped others get to the bomb shelters.

Rosalind's studies included the subject of crystallography, which was to become her area of expertise. After three years at Cambridge, the faculty offered her a research scholarship for her fourth year. For the first time in her life, she lived alone, in a rented room, where she could read, sew, and occasionally invite friends over.

In the summer of 1942 Rosalind had to decide on her next career move. She definitely wanted to do research—that is, pursue science for new knowledge. "I'm so afraid that in industry, I should find only science for money", she wrote. She accepted a position with the British Coal Utilization Research Association. This would allow her to do independent research while at the same time help in the war effort. Her project was to find better ways to use coal as a fuel. She proceeded to find out how the structure of coal changes when it is heated, and she developed theories to explain what happens. Between 1942 and 1946 she published five scientific papers, and earned a doctor's degree based on this work. One professor pronounced her research as bringing "order into a field which had previously been in chaos."

When the time came to look for a new position, a friend of a friend found her one in Paris. In February 1947 Rosalind became one of fifteen researchers working on industrial applications of coal. She learned the use of X-ray diffraction to look at the internal structure of charcoal and clay. Her investigation led to an explanation why one type of charcoal turns into graphite (as in pencils) upon heating, whereas another type does not. This difference had important industrial applications; it led to the development of high-strength carbon fibers, used today in planes and cars.

Rosalind's four years in Paris were among the happiest of her life. Her co-workers invited her to dinners and picnics, where she enjoyed entering into their discussions and arguments. One associate remarked that she spoke the best French of any foreigner he had heard. She adopted French customs and French fashions, and experimented with French cooking. On visits home, friends noticed her fashionable clothes, new hairdo, and make-up.

The French did not mind Rosalind's forthright manner of speaking, and her English friends tended to overlook it. Once, on a mountain-climbing vacation, a friend remarked that "I was driven more by my fear of Rosalind's tongue than of falling over the edge." At scientific lectures, Rosalind could be quick to point out mistakes made by the lecturer; this tended to provoke hostility. But whereas she was serious and intense about science, with small groups of friends she could gossip and tease like the others.

Rosalind's parents pleaded with her to return to England. But she loved France, and her work was progressing well. More publications enhanced her reputation as a scientist. Then a fellowship at King's College in London was offered, and she returned to England in 1951, half-feeling that this move might be a big mistake.

After World War II, scientists switched their main interest from physics to biology. Some wondered whether it was possible to use the technique of X-ray crystallography on substances from living organisms. John T. Randall, head of the physics department at King's College, was investigating this field. He informed Rosalind that the object of her research was to study the structure of certain biological fibers, especially DNA. DNA was known to reside in every living cell, as the key that governs the inheritance of characteristics from parent to child. She was given an assistant, a young graduate student named Raymond Gosling.

Randall's second-in-command, Maurice Wilkins, was away on a short vacation when Rosalind arrived. He had looked forward to having her join his team; he knew of her reputation in taking X-ray diffraction photos, but he did not know of her work with coal. Rosalind assumed the DNA project was hers alone. Wilkins thought she was simply a technical assistant, and he expected to analyze the X-ray photos that she and Gosling took.

From the beginning, Rosalind and Wilkins did not get along. Temperamentally they were opposites. He was meditative, indirect, and apt to avoid heated discussions. She was opinionated, quick to defend her views, and enjoyed loud scientific debates. Both of them worked on DNA, but separately. Rosalind felt that Wilkins was encroaching on her research territory. Once, when Wilkins suggested that they collaborate, she blew up. "How dare you interpret my data for me?" she exclaimed.

To make matters worse for Rosalind, women were excluded from the men's lunchroom and from the bar where the men often gathered after work. The atmosphere was quite different from what Rosalind had experienced in France. Her friends were limited to people outside the lab.

Within a year of her arrival, Rosalind had important clues about the structure of DNA. She discovered that DNA can exist in two forms, a wet one with elongated fibers, and a dry one. She called the dry form A and the wet one B. The two forms, when photographed separately, gave the clearest images seen up to that time. The wet form gave better pictures because water molecules separated the DNA molecules from one another; thus the X-ray beam reflected off only one molecule of DNA at a time. It produced spots in the pattern of a cross, which indicated the shape of a helix—that is, a spiral, like a spring. Rosalind believed that subunits of the DNA called phosphate sugars were situated on the outside of the helix, and other subunits called bases were on the inside. But she needed proof.

Dr. Randall tried to arbitrate the issue between Rosalind and Wilkins. Rosalind was henceforth to work on the A form, and Wilkins on the B form. But Wilkins got bogged down. He began to visit an old friend, Francis Crick, who was doing crystallography research at Cambridge. Crick had a young American co-worker named James Watson, who knew biology and genetics. These two were not working on DNA, although there were somewhat interested in it. They knew that the DNA project belonged to the team at King's College.

Someone in the United States, however, was very interested in DNA. Linus Pauling, an eminent scientist in California, proposed a helix structure. Crick and Watson persuaded Wilkins to build a model of what the DNA molecule might look like, incorporating Pauling's ideas. Rosalind thought building models was a waste of time. Only X-ray photos could show the molecular structure, she maintained.

In November 1951 Rosalind gave a talk to about fifteen scientists about her work, citing evidence for a helix. Among those present was James Watson. He had heard about "the terrible Rosy" from Wilkins, and was eager to see her himself. During her talk, he mentally criticized her clothes and her hairdo. This caused him to miss some important points she made. The following week he and Crick built their model, and invited the King's College team to Cambridge to see it. One look told Rosalind that it was all wrong; there was no place in it for water. Watson and Crick were then ordered to stop working on DNA.

Using a tilting camera that she and Gosling had designed, Rosalind's photos became increasingly sharper and clearer. On May 2, 1952, she obtained the clearest picture yet of the B form, which showed beyond a doubt a helix. She put it in a drawer and returned to the A form.

That fall, Linus Pauling's son Peter arrived at Cambridge to do research. He received a letter from his father saying Linus had worked out the structure of DNA. Peter showed the letter to Watson and

Crick. Their hearts sank. They had ignored the order to stop their DNA work, and were eager to crack the DNA problem themselves. Was Linus Pauling going to beat them to a solution?

The rift between Wilkins and Rosalind widened. They rarely spoke to each other. Wilkins wrote to Crick that "Rosalind barks often but doesn't succeed in biting me . . . She no longer gets under my skin."

In January Peter Pauling brought his father's soon-to-be-published paper to Watson. It showed a helix with three chains twisting around one another. It was like the model he and Crick had built, which had turned out to be wrong. There was still a chance that he and Crick could win the race. Rosalind, on the other hand, did not even realize she was competing in a race.

Watson appeared at Rosalind's lab to show her Pauling's paper and discuss its implications. Rosalind maintained that a helix still was not proven beyond a doubt. Watson implied she was incompetent in interpreting X-ray data. Both were in an angry mood when they parted. Watson, meeting Wilkins in the hall, poured out his feelings toward "Rosy". Wilkins then showed him Rosalind's best photo, taken eight months before, which, as assistant head of the department, Wilkins was entitled to have. He did not ask Rosalind's permission to show it, as he should have. Watson later wrote, "The instant I saw the picture my mouth fell open and my pulse began to race." It was unmistakably a helix. On his way back to Cambridge. he decided there must be two chains in the helix.

Watson received permission to build a model. His supervisors could not risk that Pauling would beat them to the correct structure. Rosalind now also tried building a model. She had come to accept that both the A and B forms were a helix with two chains. She and Watson each wrestled with the problem of how the two chains were connected. Watson realized that the bases formed the connections, like the rungs of a ladder, and that all the rungs must be the same size. The bases come in four varieties, two to a rung, but they are not randomly interchangeable; they are always paired with the same partners. Watson's intuition told him that the chains could thus separate like a zipper, and each half serves as a template to build the opposite chain. Thus the DNA molecule embodies a set of instructions to duplicate itself.

Rosalind, without knowing it, was herself within two steps of solving the DNA puzzle. But she was trained not to jump to conclusions or rely on intuition; she needed hard evidence. She had two papers on their way to publication, but Watson and Crick beat her to revealing the DNA structure in print.

Randall and his associates at King's College were furious that they had been scooped by the Cambridge group. Randall ordered his group to rush two papers to the journal before the Watson/Crick paper was published. All three papers appeared in the same issue. The Watson/Crick paper included the comment "We were not aware of the details of the results presented (in the following two communications) when we devised our structure"—a half-truth at best.

Rosalind had not been consulted on the use of her data, and was not named by Watson and Crick as the source. She must have realized that her contribution was ignored, but she did not complain. When the three papers appeared in print in April 1953, she had already left King's College, only too happy to leave the antagonistic atmosphere there.

She moved to Birkbeck College, another branch of the University of London, to work with the renowned crystallographer J. D. Bernal. Under Bernal she was to work on the tobacco mosaic virus, which produces mottled patches of light and dark green on tobacco leaves. This research was prompted by a desire to understand how a virus infects a cell. While waiting for new equipment to arrive, Rosalind took a vacation to Greece and Israel.

The Birkbeck lab was a much more pleasant place to work in for Rosalind. Bernal treated men and women equally, and encouraged women in their careers. Rosalind and her team soon became a world leader in using X-ray diffraction to determine the structure of viruses. They used the new technique of inserting a heavy atom into the tobacco mosaic virus, just as Dorothy Hodgkin had done in her work with cholesterol. Comparing the X-ray patterns obtained showed that the virus consists of protein subunits forming a cylinder surrounding a chain of RNA (a variation of DNA).

In 1954 and again in 1956 Rosalind attended conferences in the U.S. and visited American labs where work on viruses was carried out. She was impressed by the caliber of scientists she met in America. The contacts she made led to a number of collaborative papers over the ensuing years. Her spare time in the U.S. was spent hiking, swimming, sightseeing, and camping in the mountains. Her personality had softened. One scientist found her "a very sweet person, very attractive and very ladylike." She was now on friendly terms with Watson and Crick, and even vacationed one summer with Francis Crick and his wife.

At various times, friends tried introducing Rosalind to single men, but nothing ever came of these attempts. She was, however, good at entertaining the children of friends; she enjoyed playing with them, and always brought them little gifts.

At Birkbeck Rosalind gained a close collaborator in Aaron Klug, who switched to the virus project after viewing Rosalind's photos. He and his wife quickly became close personal friends of Rosalind's. Klug admired her as a scientist. "It takes imagination and intellect to know precisely what experiments to do, to design them, prepare the specimens, and then to observe the results," he wrote later. "Her single-mindedness made her a first-class experimentalist, with the sort of skill that blends intelligence and determination." Three research assistants eventually joined their team; they became like a family to Rosalind.

A pain in her stomach that began in the U.S. forced Rosalind to see a doctor on her return to England. Admission to a hospital, and an operation to remove two large lumps followed. Her parents were informed that she had ovarian cancer. She moved in with her parents to recover.

She returned to her beloved lab, but found she had only enough energy for half-days. But publications still flowed from her research team. In addition, she investigated new sources of financial support, dreading the day when her team might have to split up for lack of funding. She was asked to build a large model of the tobacco mosaic virus, to be displayed at the World's Fair in Brussels, Belgium, as the centerpiece of an exhibit on viruses. Having finished work on this virus, she next turned to the polio virus.

Her health seemed to improve while undergoing chemotherapy. If she experienced pain or nausea, nobody ever knew about it. She continued to travel to conferences abroad. But a new lump in her stomach was growing. The thought of dying before her work was finished filled her with anguish. In order to be prepared for the inevitable, she made out a will, naming Aaron Klug as the main beneficiary.

By March 1958, Rosalind was putting in full days in the lab again. She was full of plans for trips that summer. But another stay in the hospital dashed those plans. She died on April 16, at the age of thirty-seven.

An obituary written by J. D. Bernal stated that "Rosalind Franklin's early and tragic death is a great loss to science." Another obituary stated "As a scientist, Miss Franklin was distinguished by extreme clarity and perfection in everything she undertook. Her photographs are among the most beautiful X-ray photographs of any substance ever taken." It went on to summarize her contributions to coal research and to unlocking the structure of DNA and virus particles.

Watson, Crick, and Wilkins were named Nobel Prize winners in 1962. In their acceptance speeches, neither Watson or Crick mentioned Rosalind Franklin, and Wilkins mentioned her only as a passing reference. Four years later, James Watson published "The Double Helix", a book that recounts how the structure of DNA was unraveled. It became a best-seller. But scientists were aghast at how the author portrayed "Rosy" in his book; she was painted as a wicked stepmother type—hostile, uncooperative, unattractive to men, and not that good a scientist. In his grab for total credit, Watson tarnished his own reputation. After the book was published, he admitted that without Rosalind's X-ray photo, he and Crick would never have been able to decipher DNA.

Slowly the scientific world began to accept

Rosalind's real contributions, and give her the recognition she deserved. Her life was dramatized on British television. The model she constructed for the Brussels World's Fair, which was seen by 42 million visitors, was exhibited in a science museum until 1964, and after that, at Cambridge University. In 2000 King's College named a new building the Franklin-Wilkins Building; both Watson and Crick attended its official opening.

Would Rosalind Franklin have shared the Nobel Prize if she had lived? It is a question that cannot be answered. The Nobel goes only to living persons, and no more than three may share the award in any one field each year. Wilkins had seniority on the King's College staff, and therefore would most likely be favored by the Nobel committee. Not until 1982 did a Nobel audience hear any praise of Rosalind Franklin, when her co-worker Aaron Klug won the Nobel Prize in chemistry.

Rosalind did not worry that she had lost the race for DNA. She died knowing that she had made important contributions to science.

Sylvia Earle

Sylvia Earle fell in love with the ocean when she was only three. She was playing in the surf on the New Jersey shore when a giant wave swept in and knocked her down. She got back on her feet and waited happily for the next wave. This love of the ocean and everything in it determined Sylvia's career. Her daring underwater explorations led to new knowledge about the sea, and a deep appreciation of its importance in our lives.

Sylvia was born on August 30, 1935, in Gibbstown, New Jersey. In 1938 the family moved to a nearby farm. Both of Sylvia's parents had grown up on farms, and wanted the same experience for their three children. Her father Lewis Earle installed wiring and plumbing in the old farmhouse to make it a comfortable home. He added apple and pear trees to the old orchard, and planted a vegetable garden. In order to spend time with his children during their waking hours, he worked the night shift at a nearby factory.

Young Sylvia found the farm an exciting place to

explore. She could pick wildflowers, or sample berries from a mulberry bush. Sometimes she lay under the swaying branches of a lilac bush and watched ants or grasshoppers or caterpillars crawling past. Family vacations to the seashore were especially adventurous. There Sylvia and her two brothers collected seashells—shiny deep blue mussels or pale ridged cockles. Occasionally she picked up a horseshoe crab crawling ashore to lay its eggs, and deposited it back in the surf.

When she grew a little older, Sylvia liked to sit by the pond on the family's land, and write down anything interesting she saw, such as a dragonfly hovering in midair, or a catfish rising to the surface of the pond. Sometimes she caught a tadpole in a jar and brought it home, to join her collection of other small creatures.

Evenings were spent reading. Sylvia especially liked adventure stories and animal stories. Mrs. Earle was happy that her daughter loved the natural world as much as she herself did.

When Sylvia was twelve, the family moved to Florida. Her father decided to start his own electrical contracting business, and her older brother Evan, who suffered periodically from pneumonia, was expected to improve his health in the warmer climate.

Sylvia was thrilled to find that her backyard was the entire Gulf of Mexico. A new pair of swim goggles allowed her to peer through the water at small fish or crabs. Watching the marine life along the shore made her forget her initial disappointment of having to leave the New Jersey farm.

At the local library, Sylvia discovered books by William Beebe, a biologist who had invented a vessel that could descend deep into the ocean. She longed to see for herself the sea creatures Beebe described. Her ninth grade science teacher encouraged this interest in the sea.

At sixteen, Sylvia had her first underwater experience. A boy from school invited her and her brother to try out diving gear that the boy's father used to dive for sponges. Sylvia put on the heavy copper helmet that was attached to a tank of compressed air, and plunged into the river. The compressed air must be at a slightly higher pressure than the external water pressure; otherwise the weight of water above the diver would crush him or her. As Sylvia stood on the river bottom, thirty feet below the surface, she was enchanted by what she saw: a school of small orange fish, which ignored her presence, and a huge alligator gar with a mouthful of razor-sharp teeth.

The following year she had the opportunity to try

out scuba gear, a diving device that had been invented by Jacques Cousteau in 1942. She enrolled in a marine biology course at Florida State University. The instructor, Dr. Harold Humm, took his class five miles out to sea and let them jump overboard into a bed of sea grass. This experience left Sylvia wondering if she could become a teacher of marine biology like Dr. Humm. He, on his part, was impressed by Sylvia's enthusiasm and dedication to learning.

After graduation from Florida State University, Sylvia applied to several graduate schools. She chose Duke University, which offered her a full scholarship. Also, she looked forward to studying further under Dr. Humm, who was then teaching there.

In Duke's graduate program, Sylvia concentrated on the study of algae—simple aquatic plants that occur in a variety of forms and in numerous habitats. One form is the green scum that forms on ponds. Others are complex seaweeds that can grow up to thirty yards in length. Blue-green algae were among the first forms of life on earth. Many kinds of algae live in warm coastal waters. Sylvia especially liked those that can glow, like lightning bugs.

One problem that Sylvia encountered at Duke was the feeling that women were not welcome in the science departments. She wanted a position as a teaching assistant to help pay her expenses, but was told those were reserved for male students. However, faculty members got her an appointment in the university's herbarium, where plant specimens were kept. Around that time, Sylvia decided she did not want to teach; what she wanted was to be the one doing exciting explorations and underwater studies.

At twenty, Sylvia married Jack Taylor, a young zoologist. But she was determined that marriage not interfere with her goal of being a marine biologist. She undertook a complete study of the algae found in the Gulf of Mexico. For each specimen she collected, she recorded the depth at which it was found, the temperature and salt content of the water, and what animals lived among that species of algae.

During this period, Sylvia gave birth to two children: Elizabeth in 1960, and Richie two years later. Often she took the children out in her boat on her collecting trips. Sometimes they helped her place her specimens between sheets of cardboard and blotting paper.

In August 1964, a wonderful opportunity came her way. A research ship was leaving on an expedition to the Indian Ocean. One of the botanists was suddenly unable to go, and Dr. Humm recommended Sylvia as a replacement. Her husband and parents agreed to care for the children during the six weeks she would be gone.

Soon after boarding the "Anton Bruun", Sylvia realized that not all of the men welcomed her. Some still held on to the superstition that a woman on a ship brings bad luck. She knew she would have to prove herself. She rose at 5 a.m. each morning, spent most of the days underwater, and wrote up her observations in the evenings. Like a kid in a candy store, she wanted to be everywhere at once—following butterfly fish, poking at giant sea cucumbers, standing upside-down to peer at a spotted eel in a crevice. Among the creatures that she described in her journal was a red alga, new to science. A forest of them covered rocks, each one shaped like a tiny palm tree. As the discoverer, Sylvia could give it a scientific name; she chose *Hummbrella hydra*, in honor of Dr. Humm.

As the only woman aboard the ship, Sylvia became the unofficial ambassador at ports where the ship docked. In that capacity, she joined the ship's captain and chief scientist in meeting local officials.

Other scientific expeditions over the next two years took Sylvia all over the world. During this period she met Eugenie Clark, a scientist known as the Shark Lady. Here Sylvia found a role model—a woman scientist with her own lab, who was also a wife and mother. The two often went diving and collecting together. When Dr. Clark moved to New York in 1965, Sylvia took over the work of her lab in Sarasota, Florida. Studying sharks gave her a perspective on the entire ecosystem, from those at the bottom of the food chain to the predators at the top.

In 1966 Sylvia earned her doctor's degree from Duke University. Her research project on aquatic plant life in the eastern Gulf of Mexico made a splash among marine scientists.

After nine years, Sylvia's marriage to Jack ended in divorce. She and her children moved to Boston, and soon thereafter she married a fish biologist named Giles Mead, who had three children from a previous marriage. This marriage produced a daughter named Gale.

In 1969 the U.S. government started a project to study life in the sea. A team of four scientists would live for two months in a special underwater laboratory near the Virgin Islands. The government expected to learn about the problems of persons living in close proximity in an alien environment. The knowledge thus obtained would be useful in planning space exploration. When several qualified women asked to participate, the government planners asked Sylvia to lead an all-women team. Having more diving experience than any other applicant, Sylvia was a logical choice for this venture, called Tektite. Her parents again offered to keep the children. Sylvia looked forward eagerly to spending two whole weeks fifty feet underwater. Even the newspaper's calling her a housewife in its headline did not dampen her enthusiasm.

The lower level of the Tektite container was the crew's living quarters. A ladder led up to the work station. A tunnel led to the life-support system and to a ladder extending to a chamber that opened to the sea. Television cameras showed the crew's activities twenty-four hours a day—something that required mental adjustment among the women.

Sylvia's project was to study plant species growing on the reef and to see how algae were affected by fish. By the second day she had learned to ignore the prying eyes of the TV camera. The government's object of seeing how people got along in close quarters was secondary to Sylvia. Each morning the women put on their diving gear and set out, their way lit by small flashlights. A waterproof writing slate allowed each one to take notes.

Sylvia wrote, "Our sense of freedom and delight is so great that along the way we do somersaults, rolls, and loops." What was surprising was that the fish were as curious about the human among them as she was about them. Five gray angelfish followed her around every morning, as if interested in her activity. Among the most curious was a grouper, a fish that can grow up to ten feet in length. Swimming at night, Sylvia could see small creatures gleaming in the dark. Some species came out of hiding only at night. One afternoon, Sylvia used a "rebreather" rather than the usual scuba tanks. This allowed four hours of exploration at a time, rather than a single hour. The rebreather was also quieter than the scuba; it let Sylvia hear "the crunch of parrotfish teeth on coral, the sizzle and pop of a snapping shrimp, the grunts of groupers, the chattering staccato of squirrelfish."

All too soon, the two weeks were up. All four women were satisfied with their research results. Back on dry land, they found themselves celebrities. They were invited to the White House by First Lady Pat Nixon, and they were honored in a parade in Chicago. Television personalities asked to interview Sylvia, and she got many speaking engagements. Although somewhat embarrassing at first, Sylvia realized that all this attention gave her a platform to speak out, urging protection of the sea and everything in it. She was aware that toxic substances were being dumped into the ocean, causing widespread damage to the marine environment by pollution and degradation. "I'm changed forever because I lived underwater for two weeks," she said later. "I wish that everybody could go live underwater, if only for a day."

During the 1970s, Sylvia went on expeditions that took her to China, Panama, the Bahamas, and again to the Indian Ocean. She teamed up with a couple who were studying humpback whales, Roger and Katy Payne.

Whales have been hunted for centuries, but by the 1930s the numbers killed each year had increased to about 50,000. Several species of whales, including the humpback, became endangered. No one had ever swum with whales before, as Sylvia planned to do.

Offshore from the Hawaiian Islands, where the humpbacks migrate northward every spring, Sylvia slipped fearlessly into the water. Her dive partner, photographer Al Giddings, followed her down with his camera. Sylvia was interested in the forms of life associated with humpbacks, either attached or free-swimming. She found that the whales are a floating home for barnacles, the little volcano-shaped shells found on rocks below the high-tide mark, and on boat bottoms. She estimated that one whale may carry a half-ton of barnacles. At close quarters, she could see whales are also hosts to algae and to pale pink lice. In addition the whales are often accompanied by small fish, dolphins, or smaller whale species.

The whales proved to be as curious about the humans in their midst as the humans were about them. Once five whales swam with Sylvia and Al for two hours. While underwater, they often heard the humpbacks "singing"—a phenomenon described by the Paynes. The sounds are a mixture of whistles, moans, and squeals, so loud and intense that in the water they could feel the vibrations. Al Giddings was successful in filming one whale singing—the first ever caught doing that on film.

During the three months the team followed the whales, Sylvia learned to recognize certain individuals by their markings. In a narrow channel between two islands, where the wind and current kicked up huge waves, Al filmed a group of pygmy killer whales interacting with the humpbacks. Why these two species would mingle remains a mystery. Once a shark approached Sylvia; she gave it a sharp kick with her flippers, and it retreated. Such encounters did not faze her at all. "Sylvia has more guts than almost anybody you can name," said Roger Payne.

After Hawaii, Sylvia and Al Giddings set out for Glacier Bay, Alaska, where humpback whales arrive in May and June. Here they watched the whales feeding: they lunge forward, fill their mouth, then strain out the small marine creatures called collectively krill through the sieve-like plates in their upper jaw. Once the researchers watched a whale form a bubble net, to herd small fish and krill into a circle about ten feet in diameter. The whale swam in an upward spiral, releasing bubbles that rose to the surface. Then the whale surfaced in the center of the ring and swallowed its prey.

Seeing how gentle and peaceful the whales acted, Sylvia could understand how they had been hunted almost to extinction. "In less than a century we have traded sixty million years of history for margarine and cat food," she wrote. Fortunately alternatives have been found for whale meat, oil, and bone.

As Sylvia's children became teenagers, she sometimes took them along on expeditions to help the ship's crew. All had learned to scuba dive at an early age. One time she had them enter the water to experience the humpbacks' singing.

The documentary film that Sylvia and Al

Giddings made, titled "Gentle Giants of the Pacific", was shown in twenty countries. Sylvia was glad that she could share her thrill of watching whales frolicking. More than ever, she felt she had a duty to speak out on behalf of all sea creatures. A film of her walking along the bottom of the sea would help people understand the possibilities opened up by deep-sea exploration. Although this had never been done before, Al Giddings approached Sylvia with the idea. Of course she could not resist the challenge.

A diving suit had been invented by Jim Jarrett, which was used by men working on oil rigs and for underwater salvage. Sylvia, in this so-called Jim suit, would be tethered to a submersible vessel that would follow her as she walked. Funds were obtained from the National Geographic Society and other sources. The Jim suit was adjusted to fit Sylvia's small frame. She practiced walking in it, first in a large tank, and then in shallow water. Others involved in the project got nervous as the time of the dive drew closer. What if something went wrong? But Sylvia was not to be swayed.

On October 19, 1979, the small submersible sank into the Pacific Ocean off the island of Oahu. Twice they had to abandon plans for Sylvia's deep-sea stroll when a copper wire snapped and she lost voice contact with Al. The third time there were no mishaps. The submersible found a spot 1250 feet below the surface, and Sylvia staggered out into the unknown, feeling like an astronaut walking on the moon. At this depth, her suit withstood a pressure of 600 pounds per square inch, and the temperature of about forty degrees Fahrenheit made her feel like a walking refrigerator.

She found a wealth of activity all around her: crabs scurried across the sand, jellyfish drifted by, sting rays hovered, a small shark glided past. She could write down all her observations, since the Jim suit was roomy enough to allow her to withdraw her hands from the metal arms. When she asked Al to turn off the lights, she was surprised that even at this depth sunlight penetrated faintly, giving everything a blue glow. Now she could see a number of fish of fantastic shapes. As she touched a stem of a six-foot-high bamboo coral, a blue light pulsed down the length of the stem. A touch at the bottom sent a similar light rippling upward. While she was contemplating the possible purpose of this light, Al's voice came on to tell her the two-and-a-half hours were up. Before entering the submersible, she planted two small American flags in the seabed, to mark the place of this historic dive.

The results of this venture included a television

special, news stories around the world, and a book titled "Exploring the Deep Frontier". But in spite of all the publicity, money for underwater research became more difficult to come by. To counteract this trend, Sylvia and an engineer named Graham Hawkes formed a business to build small submersible vehicles. But there seemed to be no customers for such a product.

Graham Hawkes then designed a remotely-operated vehicle (ROV), useful for inspecting underwater equipment. After a time, they sold ten of these. A smaller ROV was purchased by Disney World for visitors at Epcot's Living Seas Pavilion. Customers throughout the world ordered this model to check underwater pipes, find shipwrecks, and carry out similar tasks.

In 1990 the U.S. government recognized Sylvia's leadership in sea exploration. President George H. W. Bush appointed her chief scientist at the National Oceanic and Atmospheric Administration. At first she was afraid that the position would not allow her to voice her own opinions. But she accepted the appointment. The NOAA staff were excited to have someone of her reputation. "She's greatly respected for her very broad knowledge and her ability to put it all together into one big picture—the whole marine world," said Eugenie

Clark, the shark expert. From a study of algae, Sylvia's interest had expanded to include all marine life and its relationship to other life on earth.

Sylvia's job required a move to Washington. This move was easier, now that her children were adults. She had to attend many meetings, and at times speak before Congress. But she also found time to go on expeditions. One of these was sponsored by the Japanese government. Their three-person submersible took Sylvia down 13,000 feet, or 2 ½ miles—deeper than anyone had been before.

Disappointed that the U.S. government allocated so little money to sea exploration, she resigned from the NOAA in 1992. But before leaving, she headed a team of researchers sent to the Persian Gulf to assess the environmental damage resulting from the flow of millions of barrels of oil into the sea. What she saw there was depressing. Crabs and sea birds had died in the thick layer of oil blanketing the shores and the marshland.

Her trips to other parts of the globe alarmed Sylvia also. Everywhere, ocean life seemed to be in trouble, either from pollution or from over-fishing. She felt the need to reach more of the public with her message. Lectures, films, and television appearances took up her time. In 1998 she was named Explorer in Residence at the National

Geographic Society. In this capacity she explores, conducts research, and promotes education and conservation.

In a book titled "Wild Ocean", Sylvia describes in words and photos twelve marine sanctuaries, which cover 18,000 square miles of ocean. These sanctuaries were established by Congress in 1972 to preserve sensitive areas, as a counterpart to the national park system. The credo behind setting aside such areas was expressed by President Theodore Roosevelt: "The nation behaves well if it treats the natural resources as assets which it must turn over to the next generation increased, and not impaired, in value."

Monitoring stations are important in evaluating the impact of human activity on marine sanctuaries. Fish populations are estimated by counting how many are caught in a net dragged through a known area of sea. Thousands of volunteer divers and snorkelers now help in taking such a fish census. Sometimes a fish census turns up a new species.

Sylvia Earle has made the public aware of the wonder of life in the ocean, and of the value, both economic and esthetic, of marine sanctuaries—the nation's "priceless national treasures." Much of the sea is still unexplored, but Sylvia and a handful of others have taken the first steps to rectify that.

Bibliography

Earle, Sylvia. *Sea Change: a Message of the Oceans.* New York: G. B. Putnam's Sons, 1995.

Ferry, Georgina. *Dorothy Hodgkin, a Life.* Granta, 1998

Haber, Louis. *Women Pioneers of Science.* New York: Harcourt Brace, 1979

Leakey, Mary. *Disclosing the Past.* New York: Doubleday, 1984.

Levi-Montalcini, Rita. *In Praise of Imperfection: My Life and Work.* New York: Basic Books, 1988.

Lindop, Laurie. *Scientists and Doctors.* New York: Twenty-first Century Books, division of Henry Holt & Co., 1997.

Maddox, Brenda. *Rosalind Franklin, the Dark Lady of DNA.* New York: HarperCollins, 2002.

McGrayne, Sharon B. *Nobel Prize Women in Science.* Secaucus, NJ: Birch Lane Press, 1993.

O'Hern, E.M. *Profiles of Pioneer Women Scientists.* Washington, DC: Acropolis Books Ltd., 1985

Straus, Eugene. *Rosalyn Yalow, Nobel Laureate.* New York: Plenum Trade, 1998.

Willis, Delta. *The Leakey Family.* New York: Facts on File, 1992.

Index